Table of Contents

Greetings from the author

This book is for **ADULTS!!!!**

1

Dear

Reader

Hi, I'm Greg, the author (I love saying, "author," it sounds so dignified.) You may not know me, but I can assure you with as many dating sites as I have been on your brother, uncle, cousin, father, or future divorced husband may. I have spent years wading through the muddy waters of the dating pool. I was hoping that one day "Mr. Man of my dreams" would come and make an honest man of me. Let's just say as of writing that sentence, it ain't happened yet.

We all know that dating in this day and age is depressing. Men are either too aggressive or not aggressive enough, too tall, or not tall enough. (Wait, can you ever be too tall?) Some woman out there is reading this, saying "Yes" (Shut up single bitch. That's why you need this book.). Being human, we can always find a reason to say, "Something just ain't right." (Well hold on to your nickers girls, it's going to be a bumpy ride.)

I know you are saying at this point, "Why in the hell am I listening to your dating tips and you ain't even got a man?" Well, here's where I tell you the answer, for years women especially, have been listening to other single ass, man-less women tell them how to get and get rid of a man. I'm single and Man-less. There that's the reason.

I think I have a good grasp on the man's train of thought, seeing as though I am one with a woman's sensibility. Besides, where would you women be without a gay man's advice? Hair, clothes, cheering sections at weddings and baby showers, even after we said, "Gurl.... is he the one?" We are there to support and judge at the same time.

I wanted to write this book to make you laugh and most importantly tell you how it is for twenty-five date-able years I have been able to avoid the pitfalls of finding myself in a relationship that involved the police, a restraining order, an awkward meeting with the parents with no intent on being with the man or staying in an expired situation.

I am not a doctor, so I won't go into professional jargon, I am just a human being that's able to point out the obvious in a world where we tend to walk around blindly pretending like he didn't tell you what you were too dick-matized to hear. Please remember what you do with my tips is up to you. But I write very plainly so what I'm saying is not up to interpretation "It is what it is."

Though I have just said "It is what it is.," some of you are still attempting to over complicate what I'm saying with your personal experience. Please note every situation in this book won't be the fucking story of your life. Take a page from Sam Smiths song and, "Know you're not the only one."

"Damn Greg, you don't have to be so mean." Yes, I do. I have found in my travels that because women as a whole have to be right about everything when you are talking about them. Sometimes you have to jar them into examining their behavior. Basically, make you feel an extreme emotion to get a truthful reaction then find out what the real problem is.

Seeing as though saying, "No, don't do it gurl.," is too complex for some to grasp. (Yes, I said it.) Some people can't just accept that again, "It is what it is." Sometimes you have to go into detail to show them what is right in front of their face. I intend to. By the end of this book, you might not like me, agree, or follow any of my tips and that's fine, but you will laugh, and something is inevitably going to stick.

For the men that might find this book perusing through Amazon, bookstores (Does Barns and Noble still exist?) or shelves at the last bookstore in downtown LA, "I know, why is he telling all the secrets?," because as simple as we are. We tend to make shit, so complicated, especially us gay ones. The problem is lots of us don't pay attention to emotional details. (The things that add supposed color and context to the story.)

Men tend to look at the bigger picture and not smaller components. It's the smaller components that women have been taught for eons to pick up on. Which is why rather than bullet points lots of women talk in stories. Most men are bored by too many details. So, if by chance you found this book in your girlfriend's/wives stash and you have fallen madly in love with her. Thank me later and tell her I said thank you for following my tips.

Warning if you couldn't tell by now, I cusses. (Yes, I spelled that right.) cusses. If in fact, that bothers you place the book back on the shelf and grab the one right next to this one. I'm sure they are just as good (Let me stop lying.) You will find that instead of using quotes I use parenthesis to note when I, the writer am commenting on something I just said. That is intentional. I, unlike a lot of people, find myself entertaining and I hope you do too. I'm a funny bitch.

Lastly, I must make a disclaimer because people can sue for anything even their own negligence. All advice in this book is what has worked for me and friends whose names have been changed to protect the guilty. This means if you read this and know it's you, nobody will know but me and you unless you say something, and yes, I thought what you did was smart, stupid, or just plain out of line. Thank you for the material.

Love Greg.

The biggest secret about men that women need to know is....
You thought I would just give it to you on the first page, bitch
I'm'ma make you work for this.

Gregory D Alexander

Chapter 1

Meet people as you are.

"If I was anyone else, I wouldn't have gotten laid as much."

Gregory D. Alexander

*L*ong, long, long ago, in a time of horse drawn carriages and puffy garments. They walked around in heel's makeup and lavish wig's. Proudly like a peacock. They strutted through the streets showing off their taught legs and alabaster faces accented with deep red lips and blushed rosy cheeks. "What you thought I was talking about the women. Silly, no, the men! Yes, Ladies you did not corner the market. Men did it first. It was a sign of status, stature, and nobility; however, it soon became a measure of beauty for you.

I find myself at times entranced in Facebook Reels. If I'm not watching the equally disgusting and fascinating pimple popping videos. (You know you agree.) or the beautiful muscular men with no shirt on rubbing their hands together like praying mantis's, glistening from their mothers good bottle of baby oil, I watch the makeup transformations, and let me tell you some of you are truly practicing witchery.

I don't like to call people ugly, because I think that everybody looks like something to somebody. I will say this though, "Makeup is some Harry Potter type of shit nowadays. Y'all be changing your whole face. I be like "You know that ain't her. Ain't no way in hell that's that bitch," but alas Cinderella's sisters can become Cinderella, with the aid of contouring. You can thank RuPaul's Drag Race, Mac, Maybelline, and Loreal for this.

Uneven, dry skin, brittle hair, and a waste line can be changed by one click on Amazon. These elaborate illusions have tricked, bamboozled, and straight baffled men for years. Some women have been able to maintain these facades. Waking up an hour earlier, sleeping pretty, and never allowing their mate to see what they actually look like. They not only do this with their appearance but also with their personality.

There was this story that circulated on the internet about a Surgically altered beautiful woman in Korea, I think, that married this man. To the man's surprise, after having kids the wife's original face showed up on the kids. After seeing old pictures of his wife, he was horrified. The man found out that his wife used to look like the backside of an old man with adult acne, He screamed "you fooled me! I want a divorce." (If I say that in my version of a Korean voice in my head, is it still racist?)

The man felt betrayed. Of course, he did. He thought that he was getting a beauty queen. I have an inkling that it was more than that, that made him want a divorce, but we'll just say for chapter purposes that that was it. While we are speaking on this topic, do you think that you should be required to tell someone you have had a nose job?

Somewhere down the line women have been taught they need to be subservient to a man's needs. Because of this they forgo who and what they want to be, in order to get a man. But oh no ladies, the closer you get to something the more flaws you see in it.

I'll explain. Men are very apparent. Their flaws to them are their strengths. Hell, they celebrate their flaws. I say this to say that the thing you hate most about your ex, I bet he did it the first time you met him. (Drop the mic.). Sometimes we are more enamored by the man rather than what he is actually telling us.

Women are a different story. Because of this constant need to please your man and his lack of attention to detail, the cracks in your foundation can go unnoticed for years and then like a Mexican with a ten-inch dick (Very random and out of the blue). All of your cards are laid out for the world to see. (By the way, the previous statement was not racist and not an impossibility, however... prove me wrong, Lord, I welcome it.).

Men begin to feel a sense of betrayal when you don't turn out to be who you say you are. They feel like you have tricked them into falling in love. No man wants to be tricked into falling in love, because if you think a woman can get dickmatized, a man that has fallen completely for a woman will burn down yo mama's house. I like to call it the "Intoxicating Power of the Pussy." I'll go into more detail about that at a later time.

Back to this topic. To men, women represent everything that is supposed to be loyal, true, and pure, whether they themselves are or not. So, something as simple as a hair bonnet being worn to bed can drive a man's sexual libido to careen into an early grave. Why, you ask, because when he met your representative, she was perfect. She wore the right outfit and her hair fell in all the right spots. Her puss was shaved because she wanted a man. Her eyebrows were plucked, but now she has lost her sheen.

I want to interject because as I'm writing this, some of you are saying "NO!!!!, that's not true, that's not right." It ain't right but it's the truth. You ever noticed how a man will leave you for a woman that looks just like you? Here's a little secret. She's still shiny. He believes that her on her best days is the real her, just like he did with you. This 2.0 version of you might be able to hold up the illusion longer than you, long enough to get the ring. I assure you, just wait, both of you will end up reading this book. You might even suggest it to her as you marry the "Man of your dreams."

I have a friend, we will call her Jennifer every morning Jennifer gets up; goes to her vanity, turns on the bright beautiful illuminating translucent lights and transforms from plain Jane "Jennie from the block" to Jennifer Lopez in the Green dress when she dated Puffy. (In my opinion, the best she has ever looked.) Her svelte figure is aided by numerous laxatives and her bouts with dieting.

When Jennifer does this the men swoon at her feet, and she loves it. I love this for her, she's confident and self-assured. However, like Janet Jackson between albums the weight thing, she can't keep up. (I'm not fat-shaming, truth is Janet gains weight between albums. Don't come for me.) Knowing Jennifer as I do, I know that the person under the make-up and dieting, though still beautiful, is not confident. As long as she looks like Barbara Millicent Roberts, (Barbie), she can rule the world. But when she stands in the mirror first thing in the morning, she is looking at all the things about herself she wants to fix.

I was having lunch with her one crisp fall evening, and she was telling me about this guy she had met on a dating app. I asked her to see what pictures she posted out of curiosity. As she scrolled through the heavily filtered pic's, I had to ask, "Who in the fuck is this!?." Offended by my questioning she promptly said. "That's me, Bitch!!!." I said, "Gurl that ain't the girl I'm sitting across from. My friend had fallen victim to one of the biggest crimes of them all. A computer told her what she should look like, and she fell for it, hook, line, and sinker.

Let her tell it, "It's not a big deal, it doesn't look that different." I tell you, I was looking at Halle Berry in the picture and Shaneneh in front of me, (I only used those extremes to show the extremes, Jennifer is beautiful with or without all the glitz.)

My friend had been fooled into believing that slight tweaks of her face that weren't so slight made her look better, more appealing, and more dateable. This made it harder as a friend to tell her that she was catfishing. Though the pics were based on a true story, they definitely were fictitious.

Jennifer went on to meet said man, and the date went... let's just say this.

Him: How long ago did you take those Pics on your profile?

Her: Recently.

Him: Inquisitively. You sure?

Her: Offended. What do you mean? (I hate that question. What he said was what he said, and you know what he meant.)

Him: You don't look like your picture.

They still fucked at the end of the date, but she never heard from him again. Why is that, Greg? You might ask. He wanted the Illusion. Yep, it's just that simple. Men are more prone to fall into what they think is love with what they see, not with what they have. They allow themselves to see what is amazing until they are forced to see what is less desirable.

I asked Jennifer, after she told me how offended she was, if she had of met him and he wasn't the 6'2 man that he told her he was and had been 5'6 would she had of been mad?" she said and I quote "Hell Yeah." I thought, "Well bitch, what's the difference?" I decided not to say a word. We continued our drinks, and I went home. Her filtered pics stayed up and her dating results stayed the same.

After a couple more outings and her telling me about the bad luck she was having. I broke down and asked. "Up under all that makeup and that two-hundred-dollar

16

waist trainer, whose there?" She was baffled by my question. She had unknowingly thought that there was no difference. She couldn't see that everyone she met outside of her front door met her representative. Few people knew who or what she really was.

Even though women have tried to convince the world that beauty does not matter, as they slather their faces in billions of dollars' worth of skin creams, waist trainers and red bottomed shoes. Women have only continued to push the narrative that the one thing that matters the most is what you look like. Jennifer has wrapped all she is in what she looks like. That person, Jennifer 2.0 is kind of like a car salesman.

You get to her lot, you see a beautiful car, you buy it, and as you're driving home you find out the motor was put together with rubber bands, paper clips and duct tape. As much as I love my dear friend Jennifer, she is a lemon. (No shade intended.)

Every time she spoke of these men that she had dated she talked about how they weren't what they seemed. The Gag is, she wasn't either. I told Jennifer, "Why don't you try to post pictures of what you look like without all the dazzle and see what happens? To my surprise she changed two of the pics. They reflected her natural hair, her vibrant skin and actual shape. After doing this she met Paul.

Paul is an upwardly mobile black investment banker. (I still have no idea what that means.) All she can talk about is how Paul loves every part of her. She and Paul are now engaged and expecting. I also get to see both versions of her. The down to earth, no makeup version and Jennifer 2.0. I love both of them.

Jennifer is now comfortable with being either way because she now "sees" that it's okay to not be made up and be exactly who you are. I hate that getting the man had to help her to get there, but how she got there doesn't really matter as long as she made it, right?

I believe in God, you may not, and that's fine. My thought is that he made us all differently so that we can easily be found by the person that we belong to (Yes that's right I said, "Belong to." Don't read more into it than there is.).

The moment that we begin to be something we are not; it makes it hard for your somebody to tell whether you are who they have been looking for all their life. This in turn is the reason why there is an increasing number of women who complain about the number of bad men in the world.

If you don't really like dominant men, don't act like you do.

If you don't like short men don't date them, somebody does.

If you don't like small dicks. You are not all of a sudden going to like small dicks because he treats you right. I think you get the point.

I have learned in my 20-plus years of dating that if a person doesn't like you for being you, it's not for you to be offended. People are allowed to not be interested. But, I dare you when you are rejected for just being you, to just say, "Okay thank you and move on.."

I don't want to be with anyone that doesn't want to be with me. I think that Greg is a great guy. The person that has been searching their whole life for me will think the same thing upon meeting the real me. There is someone out there that is searching for me. I and you will know when we are running to 7/11 with our old college sweatshirt some flip flops, and our hair is in a messy bun/unshaved and he just walks up and says, "wow, you are beautiful." (Insert me blushing, and phone number exchanging).

The me I am, is good enough. I hope you feel the same way about you. I'm sure the real you is just as good, maybe not better than me though, lol.

Chapter

2

I want to be fucked.

"I told him I wanted some dick. He got offended so I slept with his friend."

Gregory D. Alexander

*A*hh, sex my favorite topic. My book's that talk about sex in detail have sold the most. So, I'm saying that to say, I'm not the only horny person in the world. I am a bottom, for the less educated in homosexual behavior, "the woman" in the relationship. I'm not going to get into how terrible that sounds, but I understand that some of you just can't wrap your minds around the fact that two men fuck each other and are still men.

I digress, sexually fluid women are looked at as, thots, hoes, tramps, trollops, and toss-a-bouts. Good for a fuck but, not to take home to Mama. Yet men can sleep with every woman on the block and still be allowed to hold their heads up high and marry a very upstanding woman, hmmm? That logic baffles me.

In this chapter we are going to talk about sex and why it's so important that you know that it's okay to want, crave, and need to have it. Turn that prudish bitch off in the back of your head. I am surely going to offend her sensibility and challenge her preconceived notions of who and what she is.

Lots of people think that very sexually active people are that way due to some sort of sexual trauma. This may

22

be true for some, but others are just horny. It is a part of life to want to be touched in those very special places. Some of us just want to be touched a lot more than others.

The problem is, however, when you decide that you want to be touched you can't find someone that wants to do it constantly. With that being the case, you'll end up finding others, and year after year that amount of bodies you collect doubles and in some cases triples.

Why don't men understand that if they would just get their shit together, this wouldn't be the case. Be faithful, be working and bring the good dick home and most people would be content. The number of promiscuous women would drastically drop. Let me stop lying, women are human like men, and should be allowed to know the difference between good dick and that sorry excuse for dick that you throwing. People learn their best tricks by practice, right? No gymnast could do a triple axel thingamajig if they didn't practice.

Men don't want a hoe, but they don't want a woman that's scared of the dick. Men want an upstanding woman, but they will leave that very same upstanding woman for a woman that makes them cum in a dirty public bathroom. No, it doesn't make any sense but that doesn't make it less true.

It would be nice in a perfect world if people just came premade for you out the box, but they don't. You think I learned to be as freaky as I am from one guy. The answer is, "No." It took years of taking dick for me to know what I like and how I like it. Getting that perfect arch in your back while getting hit from the back ain't easy that first go. It takes practice.

I'm going to let you in on a little-known secret, men are stupid. Women are expected to understand that and find ways to get around it. Hey, hey, hey, don't get mad at me. What are the lyrics to "Stand by your man," again? Loretta Lynn's song was a product of its time but still a sentiment for many people in the world today.

I think that the first step to understanding the truth about our male led civilization is to admit that men came up with it and women have followed it for eons. This makes you and your foremothers a part of the problem, either willingly or unwilling.

For example, some man, somewhere said that after a husband dies, a woman should go to a room somewhere in one of her children's homes, wither away and so should their pussy. So, let's make sure this is clear. If a wife dies a man is expected to remarry. If a husband dies a wife is ex-pected to die alone hopefully sooner than later.

There are two very crazy things going on here un-derneath the surface.

One: It perpetuates the notion that men cannot continue to take care of themselves without a woman pre-sent.

Two: Once a woman's husband dies her purpose as a woman is don and has come to an end.

Side story: I had this ex whose father had been dead for two decades and when I asked, "was his mother da-ting?" he got offended and said, "Why does she need to date she has 5 sons, we are all she needs.". How sweet, right? Wrong. This man was dead serious about what he said to me. I should mention he was Nigerian, and they tend to play by a different set of rules, which is the reason why we ain't together.

This man's mother was supposed to never know the pleasure of good dick again. He and his brothers were going to make sure of it. Like a wall of cock blockers. (If we had of worked out, I would have snuck her to a strip show or two, she seemed like the type.)

In many cultures the usefulness of the woman is done when the things that make her, young, beautiful, a cook, a wife, a mother have come to an end. Nobody ever remembers that she was someone before she belonged to someone else. It doesn't help that she aids in perpetuating this stereotype by not regaining herself.

Hiding in the background and silently living as if your job as a person is done is "no bueno." You are worthy of a second chance at happiness, whatever it looks like. If that's a string of flings and dates for drinks and that's it. Guess what, you can do it. Always be honest about your intentions because men be weird. But live a little. A second chance is God saying, "I love you enough to give you a do-over."

With women's lib and the absolute need for women to be able to support themselves, things are different. Women no longer need a man to be validated. We find this notion more prevalent in the African American community since Black women have been a part of the workforce since before it was considered a workforce.

Black women have been forced to take care of whole households where they couldn't even sit at the dinner table. Then due to migration and lower wages made by their men, Black women were forced to work menial degrading jobs just to help feed their starving families.

Women decided to carve out their own roads and lay their own bricks. When their husbands went to various wars, it made them have to step up. This was a woman's time to shine, and they did. The problem is that right after the husbands returned they had to get back into a woman's role. You don't give someone a taste of freedom, then tell them to go back to hanging laundry. That dear reader was the birth of women's liberation. Now everybody's the same, well.

Just like men, when women get home from a long day at work. They don't want to be bothered by your trivial issues. They are mad at the boss for some reason, and they just want to eat and get some dick. (Sounds vulgar right?). Did you know men talk like this with each other? That's why men and hookers are mentally happier than your sour puss ass, so just keep reading.

I said all that to say women have made monumental strides in the world, changing the narrative of how they should be viewed and treated. Women are now more vocal about being satisfied, and what is the best way to make sure your satisfied? The answer is to ask for it.

I have a friend; we'll call her NahNah. From what I hear, NahNah got that Ill-NahNah. I only know that because she makes sure that everyone in our friend circle knows it. NahNah is a very sexually liberated woman. It's because of her I now know how to make a man nut in 2 minutes. (Thank you gurl, It works).

NahNah has been with 130 men exactly over the 20 years that she has been having sex. (She keeps track.) She has not had one virus, disease, or abnormal growth. And other than the fact that she would rather be in a committed relationship, she's a pretty happy woman.

NahNah met a guy at a party one night in Hollywood. NahNah was at this very exclusive after-hours joint and thoroughly enjoying herself when this man who was tall, dark, a strong-looking piece of chocolate approached her. NahNah was blinded by the snugness of said stranger's pants and how revealed the enormous python he was hiding.

Him: What's good?

Her: I'm thinking that dick is.

The man backed up looked down at his pants and said, "Oh you that kind of girl.," then walked away. Nahnah spent the rest of the night wondering what kind of girl she was.

Later that weekend, she met me for lunch. We were working on a project together when she asked me "Do you think I'm a hoe?" I jokingly said "hoe-ish, not a hoe.," I didn't know at the time that my comment would cause her to rethink her life. I was just joking, hell, I probably have slept with more people than her, but she was distraught. (Remember the power of words.)

That night she had decided that she would give her life over to the Lord. She was determined to be a different person, hoping to erase NahNah and become Natalie. Natalie decided that it would help her if I came along one day on her first-ever visit to a church. I had not been to a church in 20 years and the last time I went it was nothing like this.

NahNah's one of those types of girls that lives the wildlife at night but during the day, she's kind of bland. What I'm trying not to say is... it was a white church and not just white but whiter than white. When we left I needed to watch an episode of "Good Times" and "What's Happening Now" to feel Black again.

NahNah had felt like she had found her home. I was a little leery though. When you have known someone as long as I have known NahNah You really want to believe that they want to be different. But you wonder what was wrong with who they were in the first place. It's the real friend in you that just wants your friend to be happy.

I agreed to go with NahNah the next Sunday because I didn't want her to be the only Black person in the room. Okay, to be honest, I was really praying for a new job and felt if I asked for it in a church, God would be more merciful. (I don't claim to be perfect.).

As we sat in the church, NahNah closed her eyes and fell into what looked like a trance. I don't know what she was feeling so much because the preacher worked better than a Tylenol PM. I could have fallen asleep right there in the aisle and by the sound of the man across from me snoring, obviously he had had the same idea.

Suddenly this ebony God sat down next to me and Lord my insides started to wonder, what would our children look like. NahNah started to sniff as if she smelled something then smiled. She opened her eyes and looked at me, then past me. Believe it or not the ebony God that sat next to me was the same guy from the afterhours.

Both of them looked at each other like they had both been guilty of something. After church I went to the bathroom and NahNah decided to confront the Ebony God. She wanted him to know that she was different. She was someone of value. Not just a dick hungry woman on the prowl at a club.

As I walked out of the church into the parking lot I looked around for my friend. I called her on the phone and got no answer. I walked to my car. As I attempted to call her phone again. I could hear her ringtone going off in a nearby foggy windowed jeep. She was a dick hungry woman on the prowl at the church.

After NahNah fucked the Ebony God, church was no longer a thing. (Did I just put church and fucked in the same sentence? Don't act like people don't be fucking at church y'all seen the video.) She was back to her old ways.

31

Bland days and lively nights. I was fine with the not going to church thing, because I didn't get the job. (I was overqualified) But I found it very odd that she was able to just go back to normal. First she was upset because a man assumed she was a hoe, wanted to change her life and when she slept with the man she felt like her life was just fine.

Me, NahNah and Jennifer had decided to spend the day at the most magical place on the planet. I, however, was not feeling the magic. I could not get over the NahNah thing. We sat down after getting way too expensive snacks from the concession stand, I couldn't help but ask Nahnah, "Why did she sleep with the guy knowing that he thought she was a hoe?" She looked at me and said, "I wanted to." When I slept with him, he became the hoe too. I felt vindicated. I had no idea how diabolical NahNah's mind worked.

It was at that point that I found out that I was an unwitting pawn in a game that she had come up with. After the man had kind of accused her of being a hoe, she asked around to find out his name found him on Instagram, saw what church he attended waiting to find him there and fuck him. Whereas I would have left said, "fuck you," and kept it moving. NahNah had developed a plan to prove that she would not be judged by a man.

The terrible thing is that in the eyes of others she would still be looked at as a hoe, but in her mind she was doing her, and that was all that mattered. She really didn't give a fuck about what he thought about her. NahNah was playing the long game she wanted to prove that she had the upper hand.

The whole situation taught me a few things. First don't fuck with NahNah, cause she be on some FBI shit and secondly NahNah was really not afraid of herself. If a man had of walked up to a woman and did what NanNah did people alike would not have given it a second thought. But because a woman did it, she was a hoe.

Something so natural as sex between two consent-ing adults can hold so much weight, for women that is. A man can freely throw his penis net out in the dating pool collecting all kinds of shellfish and lose barnacles knowing that his reputation will never be tarnished. You, however over 20 years sleep with two men at two separate times who just happen to be friends and you will be labeled with the scarlet letter for the rest of your life.

Now I'm not here to argue whether it is right or not that this happens, I am here to say that it does and give you a way to get around it. The way is to not give a fuck, NahNah didn't. NahNah was able to take her power, even if it was just something within herself that she needed to prove.

NahNah knows the secret that some of you refuse to understand. If it ain't right, it ain't always my job to fix it. Most people after a certain age are stuck in their ways and refuse to be different. Why are men the only ones that don't have to just take what is offered?

Like all pussy feels different all dick ain't the same and sometimes you can be bamboozled by the man into a horrible dicking. For years women have just put up with it and tried to work around it because of what the optics were. Fuck the optics. I say test the product before you get duped. You wouldn't go to the car lot and not have a test drive, would you?

For all you women out there that are now saying that you wouldn't do that. Let me tell you this, no man is going to be with you and be faithful if yo pussy whack. There I said it. And all it takes is one fuck for him to find that out. Yet you been with this man for 10 years, and he ain't made you nut once. And that's the least of his problems. (You around the house sitting under bathtub faucets and on top of washing machines like a damn fool.)

Do yourself a favor go out and test the waters. A bad sex life can lead to lots of troubles down the line. It can also lead you to lust for things that you never thought of before. This is why women be finding out that they really liked girls in their later years and feeling guilty about it. (Speaking of why is it that women seem to be finding out they like girls later than men find out they like guys? Just something to think about.)

When you get serious with someone make sure that you are honest about your sexual needs. I like a big dick, thick and long. I want you to get to the end of the hallway and paint all the walls. I could not find myself in a situation where I was with a man with a little dick. Men are either one or two ways about their dicks size, boastful or they heavily avoid the question.

Example Question

You have a big dick?

Acceptable answers are.

1. yes

2. no

3. It's small but I know how to get the job done. (He eats and it's probably better than the dick.)

Unacceptable answers are.

1. I never measured it. (We all have.)

2. I don't get no complaint's (nor do you get second's)

3. it ain't all about dick size. (Yes it is.)

There are more unacceptable answers, but these are the more frequent.

I am a fan of a good dick pic. Society has conditioned the weak minded into believing that the dick is ugly and the look of it is unnecessary for an arousal. If you're reading this book, you, and I both know that's a lie. Sucking a pretty dick can be so much more pleasurable then sucking an ugly one. Don't be afraid to want to see it. Even if you don't plan at that very moment to do something with it. At least at that point you will know what you're looking forward to.

DO NOT!!!!! let others dictate how you want to live your life. Be safe with any of your activity but be free to enjoy. The old lady in the mother-in-law room in the back of the house is now the CEO of her own business, holding down the home and the workplace and still finding time to continue to get the dust knocked off her coochie. Unlike her male counterpart all she needs is a lil lubrication and not a blue pill.

This new age woman is not living the sexually suppressed life of her foremothers. When she wants some dick, she knows exactly how to just ask for it. I applaud this lady. I aspire to be just like her. She is a marvel of the world and should be looked at as such.

So, in conclusion the next time you see a man across the room, and he approaches you with a full-on dick print and a look in his eyes that says I would fuck you until yo pussy squirts on my dick. Feel free to say "You wanna fuck?" with no shame if that's what you really want.

Disclaimer

I am in no way saying that you should sleep with every man that you come across just because its available. You should make sure to be informed and safe however you decide to proceed. I just want you to know it's okay to be horny whenever you are horny.

Chapter

3

The big boy that eats.

"He said he was hungry. I told him to come back to bed."

Gregory D. Alexander

I'm from Detroit, and in Detroit it gets cold. Like bears the people of Michigan tend to pack on the pounds during the winter. Weight, unless grossly morbid, and even in that case is not that big of a deal. Living in southern California is different. People here act like they have never seen a person over two hundred pounds. If you are over two hundred you are looked at like a zoo animal. You are hit with a barrage of gym flyers and diet concoctions that seem to work at first but then not so well.

Living in a city that truly says that your worth is purely valued by how you look can be a daunting experience. The silver lining is that big men eat pussy and ass like it's their calling. Oh, you thought I was going to tell you about some boring "I dream to be skinny topic." Some I'm depressed because I'm bigger topic? Hell no, this book is about telling you how to get what you want." This chapter is going to be ruff on skinny men, hard on muscular men, and good to the thicker of the three.

I have never had a skinny man eat my ass the way I like. Most skinny men in general eat a lot because they have fast metabolisms that cause them to burn calories faster. You would think that that would reflect in their sex. I have found in my experience that ain't the case.

Muscular men though good to look at are either too stiff or too self-involved to do what needed to be done. They tend to be more worried about the angle that makes them look the best than where the spot is to tongue fuck you to make you cream.

Big/thick boys. The bigger the better. (Side note while writing this I am sitting in a diner on sixth and Spring eating one of the most amazing pieces of sweet potato pie I have ever had in my life. I know you're like why does that matter, but like I said it was a FUCKING side note. Get over it.)

Thick boys across the Midwest and East Coast have been the most well-kept guarded secret. Their extra pounds have provided warm hugs, cuddles, and more than able tongues for centuries. Yes, that's right. They can eat, eat, eat, and in some cases snatch yo sole without even putting their dick anywhere near your cooch.

I know it's very hard to believe this but just like some of you don't like to lick pole there are some dudes out there that don't like to lick the hole. Those guys I like to call the "starved ones" they have a strict diet of fucking and maybe some kissing and that's it. Because they are just there to get a nut. The passion behind the action and the stroke is lackluster.

Spotting men that don't like to eat is easy, because they tend to tell you right off the bat that ain't their thing. You don't want to force these types of men to do it either, because I can assure you they won't be good at it, and you won't want them to do it again. You are not the only one that can give some dry ass head ladies.

Men who eat tend to have a fascination with the particular thing that they are eating. They enjoy the flavor, the feel, and the shape. They are connoisseurs of their preferred meal. They are the type of men that don't need you to do anything or be in any crazy position. They just want to put their face in it any way that they can. I love these men. These are the type of men that eat pussy/ass like it is a delicacy. (When you look back or down at them all you see is pussy/ass juices all over their beard and face and they love it.)

I have a friend we'll call him Justin. Justin is a very slim very fit late thirty-something, gay man. Justin is the kind of date you don't invite out to eat. He will order a whole side of the menu and down it with no problem. I was feeling generous and decided to invite Justin to lunch when he in turn ordered the biggest most expensive thing on the menu. (How rude.) But how LA.

While we ate, I and Justin began to talk about the crazy weather we were having and how it made him miss the dudes in Chicago. He like I am from a cold weather state and were a fan of the thicker man. (If we were both bottom's we couldn't be friends.) "All the men here are skinny and homeless or addicted to drugs.," He said. I laughed and agreed because he ain't lying.

In a city based on looks, those that don't fit the cookie cutter mold get discarded. This made me think, had I gotten so wrapped up in what the look was that even I stopped seeing my plus sized kings?

As we left the lunch, I was one hundred dollars poorer and perplexed. Why might you ask? Let me tell you. Because I, a professed chubby chaser had stopped seeing the chubby dudes. I myself had alienated the very men that I like. I was becoming an LA gay.

I looked here and there and all I saw were muscular ripped, skinny joggers running in the bike lane with flimsy too short shorts on that barely covered their kibbles and bits. I was appalled, taken a back, dumbfounded even. All the "little something extras" had gone away with beards and Myspace.

As I walked home in full-on tears, I couldn't help but wonder "Where the fuck did the fat men go?" Was there some fat boy abduction? Was I not big enough to be abducted? At 230 lbs., I know I was no longer a twink, so where did I fit. It was all so jarring.

I decided to do what all guys did when they live in LA. I joined the gym. People join the gym in the wintertime because they have hopes that by summer, they will have the body of their dreams. I went because I figured what better way to find a fine, thick dude that I could corrupt and convince to get to stay at the right thickness and love me?

The moment I sat on the exercise bike I knew that I had made a mistake. There were no thick dudes there. I had obviously come too late and caught all the thick dudes in transition. My heart began to hurt. My ass would never be eaten right again. What was I to do? It was getting cold, and I had no cuddle pillow. I was devastated.

When you come from a cold state you know the importance of having you a big cuddle bear when the weather drops below fifty. This whole moment in my life had made me realize how long it had really been since I had shared my bed with my actual type of man. I know your like "What do you mean?"

Let me ask you, do you always for the most part sleep with your type of man, or the man that you have allowed TikTok to tell you is who you should be sleeping with? I bet if you honestly have answered that question, you will realize the answer is you sleep with what society says is acceptable. Oh, you thought that you dictated those to whom you were outwardly attracted?

Let me give you an example. Because we live in a world where a lot of gay men are still afraid to be who they are they will forgo a great relationship with a fem guy just because they do not want the world to assume that they are gay, even though there is this one fem guy that under any other circumstances they would have wifed. Crazy you might say but true.

There are more examples of this in the straight world. Like a man can be with a good woman but because she is less than attractive, he will not date or bring her in public because he does not want to face public shame. (Now that was a kind of bad example because truthfully men will fuck anything. Don't let them fool you. I've seen a video of a man sticking his dick between a mattress and box spring, anything.)

As the weather dropped down even further, and my "He-pussy" was going dry, I needed to find a big man, and quick. Long gone are the days of Craigslist dating ads, (thanks creepy lady killers), so where are they I thought. I sent out a batman beacon "BIG BOYS, MY HE-PUSSY IS LOOKING FOR YOU." When I was younger, that's all I needed to do, but those young hormones that I once had now were old whore-moans to the ears of all who listened. Needless to say, nobody answered. I wanted a big boy bad.

About two weeks later, I had discovered Justin had found a job. I forced him to invite me out for lunch, in which I blamed him for all the distress that our previous conversation had caused in my used-to-be simplistic life. Then he dropped the bomb on me. The reason he got the job was because he had met this thick boy at the club one night and they had been "bumping ugly's" for a week and a half now. The traitor, I thought. If I had to suffer this big boy shortage alone, he should too.

Truthfully, I was incredibly happy for him, but yet, my bed was still empty and I long for the tongue of a real hungry man. Justin needed to leave abruptly but not before he picked up the check. (Not on my watch you greedy bitch). As I sat alone at the table still polishing off my B.L.T. and cold French fries, I decided that I was driving myself

45

crazy thinking about and hoping to find this Winston Duke of my own.

Winston Duke for those that don't know who he is, plays M'baku of the Jabari tribe in the Black Panther films, and he was the father in Jordan Peels' "Us." In my opinion, he has the perfect face, body, oh and down to that healthy chocolate tone that glows like the sunshine over an African grassy field. (No shade but it would be a true shame if he had a small dick, he's Caribbean though so I doubt it.).

Those who are really, truly into thick Adonis's will more than likely agree he is right there at the top. The thought of him massacring my innards makes my body shake just typing it. I don't know if Mr. Duke is gay, but dammit if he is, lord please let me get the chance to ride that horse. (I would suck him til the chocolate fall off.)

I decided to go about my day and just allow the world to bring me what it had for me and not what I wanted from it. You do know that never works right? The takeover spirit in us always wants to direct the activities in our lives the way that we want them to go.

I kept at it, I'm not a quitter. I tried my last viable option A4A. Some of the gays are reading this book and thinking "the phonebook? How old are you?" old enough to be on the ground floor of A4A. I have had an A4A account longer than some of these twink's have been alive. For us older gays, its where we are sure to find a suitable gay our age. You know that older gay that just doesn't want to make the jump to the more modern apps?

With today's apps we can easily get lost in the shuffle of greased up amateur prostitutes. A lot of us stay on A4A, because it's just straight forward, you see, you like, you fuck, and you may even date. Ultimately, you break up but at least you gave it a good college try.

A4A was teaming with the once hot shit dad bods I was looking for but also a whole lot of scammers. I was not interested in the selection enough to weed through the scams. Was I going to have to go to a club? The LA night club scene is not very afro-centric and though I am open, I do prefer a beautiful Black man.

You ever been to a party and once you got there felt like you should have been there to chaperone. There were twenty somethings everywhere kissing random strangers and tooting powdered things up their noses from dirty painted fingernails. This generation is troubling.

There were guys my age with that predator, I want some young meat, look in their eyes that used to creep me out when I was in my twenties. What there wasn't was, a thick tall cutie for me to throw this thirty-two, (okay damn reader thirty-five, oh you found my birth certificate and you are threatening to out me if I don't get honest. Forty-three, okay you happy? Some secrets only you and your doctor should share.) All and all there was nobody to throw this forty-three-year-old ass on.

I did see my friend Justin there sitting alone in the corner nursing an overpriced beverage. I walked over to my friend who looked down into his cracked screen phone where he was trying to find a date on Jackd. No doubt his relationship of two weeks had hit the skids. By the look of his cup of melted ice, he probably no longer had the job either. "Awe what happened?" I asked with sympathetic eyes and a joyous heart. (I was not the only single bitch in the world again.)

Justin explained that in a fit of weakness his big boy boss offered to eat his cookies and he couldn't resist so that very same night he went to the man's house and let him devour his man parts. What Justin didn't know is that the boss and the new beau were roommates. This made for a very colorful walk of shame. I was filled with rage. Not only did this idiot have one big man but then turned around and found another in the same house. I was still man-less.

That winter there was no one there to eat me like an ice cream sundae on a hot summer day. There was no cuddle season and that damn big boy trend was all the rage on TikTok no thanks to KeKe Palmer and SNL. My rabbit hole of misery had reached new levels. But you know there is always a light at the end of a tunnel.

No this is not where I tell you I met this thick boy and he has changed my life and we are spending the winter trapped in his home under a sheet because no blankets are needed, no. This is the point where I tell you I still ain't found a good eater and a big boy to take care of my inner feminine needs. But I wish that I had.

Folks let's just admit it. Though we want to be all deep and meaningful it really does come down to the little things. Those little things seem to take precedent in the end. If you like your ass/pussy ate and it brings you the maximum amount of pleasure, why would you be with someone that doesn't do it or do it right?

I'm sure I don't have to tell you that all big boys do not eat. But those that do, do it well and they're pretty cool to rub up next to. Listen, if you don't want one, just send him my way. I'll make an honest man of him.

49

(Side note: Months after cuffing season ended a 6'4 320lb big boy lifted me on his shoulders and had me grab the crown molding in my apartment, while he ate the kitty like the last supper for a man on death row. Just like God, He may not come when you want him but he's right on time.)

Chapter

4

It's Black it's White.

"I like my white men like I like my food, with a lot of flavor."

Gregory D. Alexander

A long time ago, well not that long ago, the thought of mixing races was frowned upon on both sides of the fence. During the 70s however white women at Wood Stock discovered that Darryl had more dick and rhythm than Darrin and the explosion of mixed couples happened. Okay, that's a lie, they knew our dicks were bigger long before that, and they have been mixing and mingling with us since they landed their luxury cruise ships in Africa and asked us to join them on their "three-hour tour, a three-hour tour" to a new and beautiful place called freedom land. (I type that with a sly smile.)

The appeal of the Black moist pussy and Black Mandingo dick have both excited and plagued the Whites since the days of unpaid human labor. This has caused them to run in fear but stop in curiosity. You might ask, "Why is this? What is this you speak of?" As someone who has slept with a few Whites I can tell you in my experiences with white gay men they tend to be more about the fact that their sleeping with a Black person more than the fact that they are just sleeping with a human being.

This sexual taboo excitement in them is just weird. It's like a farmer in a desolate area that's just discovered you can buy a whole female doll online and fuck her like she's real without all the complaining and "I have a head-aches.." (Gross right. Not so much. I'll talk about women's fear of being replaced later.)

It is all about being objectified. Hearing the phrase, "Give me that Black pussy.," from a White man. Ewe, gross. I feel like my ancestors are saying, "How could you? He had to force me." They are humping away on top of you like you are a mannequin at Macys.

The sex is like they are living out some creepy slav-ery fantasy that they have had since their past life. "You want this White Cock." (Oh God, I just threw up in my mouth.) Those are the worst words ever uttered by any man during sex. "No, I do not. The word "Cock" is an instant buzz kill. If we were about to fuck, we definitely ain't fuck-ing now.

Race should never play a part in something so sa-cred as sex. Yet and still, it does. Race can be the difference in behavior towards a future partner, family drama, and so-cial status. Being seen with someone of another race can drive some people to lose their ever-loving minds. It's about how we are programmed in society.

Some White and Black people's minds are still stuck in the 40s and some other ethnicities are just too far gone in their culture that they themselves don't even realize they are full blown racist. (Before I go here, I wanna say that nothing applies to everyone, but some things apply to a lot of people.)

During the covid years we were hearing a lot of Asian hate and racism things on the news. The Asians were saying they were being targeted for hate crimes and they wanted minorities to stand with them and stop the hate. "HMMMMMMMMMMM." This was so perplexing to me because the history between Blacks and Asian's has been scarred with racism and prejudice.

Most Asian countries are very much so, not Black friendly. Hell, some of them don't even like the dark skin of their own ethnicity. You think they are wearing those face shields for fashion. News flash they don't want to get darker.

The truth is as a Black person in this world dealing with racism is everywhere. The media has sold our existence as criminals complainers and lazy. Hell, we worked for free for over 300 years. You don't think we deserve a break? You don't think that we put in our dues?

I was watching a TikTok this morning about a black lady who worked in Napa as a sommelier. She was in her car after she had been fired in favor of a White woman. We live in such a society that even if that wasn't the truth, I don't doubt it. Things like this happen so regularly that we have become immune to the thought that she could have slapped the shit out of the boss and slept with his wife and we would still believe what she said because it's on task for White people. The reason for this is that Whites have done this to us for years.

All the years of mistreatment and disregard have played a huge role in how Black people see the world when dealing with White people and how we interact sexually. It's believed that White men lack the passion due to their need to be superior. As someone who has slept with a few White men I have rarely been in a situation where the fact that I was Black didn't come up. (You telling me you like Black guys only tells me that you fetishize me. I want you to just like me, not the color of my skin.)

Black men in general tend to be more passionate, (I don't have to worry about hearing the word Black.) and I don't mean with kissing and hugging, I'm purely talking about the act of the stroke. There is something about the way that we feel when our bodies collide with each other that is just plain rhythmic. Black men have worked hard at this talent of theirs. So hard that not being good at it could be devastating to their ego.

I have been led to believe that the worst thing you can do to a Black man sexually is tell him he can't fuck. It does something to their mental state. They first go on the defense because to them, it must be something wrong with your ass/pussy. It couldn't be that his stroke game is whack, but then when he is at home groping his little man in bed while watching porn, he begins to study how the guys are doing it because he realizes that he just might not be that good. It's all about doing a good job and getting praise for it.

I think that all men just want to get a nut really, however some men are better at making it good for you. Disclaimer: I'm not saying all White men or Black men are anything but those that know, know, and we all know.

White men, though the rhythm may be off aren't too bad in the big-dick category. The problem is, it's like a box of chocolates, you never know what you're gonna get. See for most when you meet a Black man you have more confidence that he gon serve up a monster when you meet a White man you like, "he might, or he might not?." I have been in some cases pleasantly surprised and in others abso-lutely horrified. (The thought of sleeping with a man with an itty-bitty dick makes me sick to my stomach. Just being honest.)

I have come to the realization that I have a type. If I'm going to date a White man he cannot be a "White Man." I know your like, "What????" (Again, those who know, know. For those that don't of course I'll explain.) Your average, run of the mill suburban White boy, just won't do. I am too Black for that. The clash of cultures would be epic, and I can't control my mouth or facial expressions. Yo mama, daddy, grandparents uncles and aunties can all get it.

When it comes to really White people, the new generation may be all peace, love, and sunshine, but I bet there is a greater portion of your family that would definitely hang a nigga if they could and probably already have.

Black peoples ears have become very sensitive to subtle racism and don't get me started on the white passive-aggressive behavior. You know what, let me get started, "You guys are aware that we do know what you mean when you say "homeboy" or you say something wrong without really saying it, right?

Your micro aggressions are met with attitude because you have just attempted to toy with our emotions.

57

And the things that Black people don't like the most is for their time, Mama, mind, energy, money, man, woman, car, or family (Even if they don't fuck with them.), to be played with.

Have you ever noticed when you are in public and Tommy is being a little shit to his mom and she is falling apart a Black person would be the first to not just speak, but step up, cause we don't play that?

The moment Tommy's lips flap open disrespectfully we in our head have already commenced to an ass-whoopin. If it happens to you in public this is how you will know your child had experienced a mental ass whoopin. "Gurl, nah see. If you hear that phrase, we about to grab yo child and beat the respect back in his ass. Don't bring your disrespectful ass kids into the hood Walmart.

I say all this to say that we are different. Same planet, same time, different culture and though ours has been heavily influenced by theirs we walk differently. Except there is "one" exception. The elusive Black/White Boy. You've seen him before in the hood his name normally starts with "White Boy" Rick, Steve, John. This is the White man that has grown up around Black people all their life and became just another nigga.

There's something special about this White boy, White girls don't want him, and he don't want them. Black girls however know that this ole Jon B, looking fine ass mutha fucka can get it. He looks like he can fuck and has good credit all at the same time and because he has been in the hood all his life you ain't got to explain a damn thing.

I have this friend I'll call her Nikita; Nikita is a mother of two who married early and divorced quickly. Up to that point Nikita had only had eyes for professional Black men. But after her whore of an ex, she now was a little more open. She tried Mexicans but found them to be too short. Arabs too restrictive, Asian's where is the meat? A White man "Oh hell No" Nikita is one of those pro Black people, the kind that if she sees a White girl in the hood jogging, says "There goes the neighborhood."

Nikita is also an author and has written many books on the gentrification of America. I love her to death, but I still feel that sometimes she goes too hard. She once cursed out the barista at Starbucks because she asked for a Black coffee and the woman put milk in it. Her reasoning was and I quote, "The White man is always trying to interject themselves in places they are not needed or wanted.," (Bitch it's just milk).

Nikita is one of those friends that you have to know exactly where you are going because it can potentially get ugly. You have no idea how many establishments I have had to apologize for her going overboard. (I would be lying if I were to say I don't take any enjoyment in it. The girl is a blast.)

She and I were in Target picking up some last-minute gifts for Christmas one year and she met Corey. She actually bumped into Corey with an arm full of Target special granny panties, her idea of a perfect gift. My idea of "Bitch what's this?"

"Damn you too fine to be wearing granny panties." Corey said as Nikita's actual panties started to melt down her leg. Corey was essentially the finest Black/White boy she or I had ever seen. Tall, well built, Italian, faded cut, perfect smile and straight out of Compton demeanor. Why could he not be pitching for my team? (The nerve of him to be straight.).

Nikita asked, what are you mixed with?" (How rude, right?). "I'm White, I ain't mixed with nothing." You had to hear how this man said, "I'm White." It was like "nah nigga, stop playin.," and remember Black people hate to be played with. He confirmed by pulling out a picture of his parents who were very much so White. Nikita shut down upon receipt then he said. "My skin White but my dick Black then a mutha fucka." I must have creamed down my leg. As gross as that may have sounded to some of you. You had to hear it. When we left, I had to call somebody's son to take care of my situation.

Needless to say, Nikita went home with Corey, and he proved that the dick was as Black as he said it was. The next time I saw Nikita there was a different heir about her. The confident, strong, Black queen seemed perplexed, lost, distracted, and baffled. It was like she could not reckon with the fact that a White man had made her feel better than any Black man had in her entire life, including her daddy, (No, not in a nasty way. Get your mind out the gutter). I mean as far as security.

Nikita went on to spin a tale of passionate sex and true oneness. "I never knew love like this before.," her words not mine. (Actually, Stephanie Mills, I give credit where it's due.). I marveled at her glow and her inability to speak one sentence without uttering Corey's name. "He really put it on you?" I said then she answered, "I truly think that I'm in love.." It had only been a week and she was already wrapped in the cocoon.

I wanted to tell her she sounded ridiculous, but if I did it would of all been out of jealousy and so I decided not to put myself out there like that. I had met nothing but duds in my journey and this bitch bumps into prince charming at the Walmart. She don't even like White dudes. What kind of all-out shit is this?

I smiled and put on my best supportive face. Hoping that the cracks in my foundation could not be seen. I think that at this point I need to tell you about how anti-white this chick is. Nikita was born in a very small town in south Georgia. Her parents owned a farm. White folks basically stole the farm from her father who was the illegitimate son of the landowner who so happened to be, yes you guessed it, White.

Nikita's family never forgave White people for what those "White devils" did to them and vowed to topple the whole system of oppression, one White person at a time.

Nikita was well on her way to overthrowing White oppression until just one week ago. (This chapter is now called how White dick can change Nikita's life, just joking.) If White dick could make this Angela Davis like Pro Black woman a sympathizer, I want to try it. Actually, I have, and it didn't have the same effect.

As the weeks went on and Nikita and Corey began to see more of each other there was a noticeable change in Nikita's attitude and appearance. She was a lot less militant, she was wearing straight hair, a feat she had not attempted since her days in college, when she decided that that was just the White man's way of making the Black woman more palatable.

"Are you okay," I asked? I was truly worried about my friend. She had developed this nervous laugh that was new to me. It was as if she had lost all her strong Blackness and became what she had always thought that White women were.

My mother had not been a stranger to dating outside her race, so I decided to ask her if she had any ideas as to what might be happening. When I asked her the first thing that she asked me was "How's their relationship?" To my knowledge, it was going well. Then I remembered throughout our conversation she kept checking her phone as if she were expecting a call that never came. Something was fishy. "I think your militant friend thought that she had to change, went too far, and is losing her man. When a White man wants a Black woman he wants her because she is Black not because she can imitate being White. If he wanted a White woman he would be with one."

My mother's words sat with me all night. The changes in Nikita's attitude in the eyes of any other Black person could be seen as White washing. Fuck that it **was** White washing. The bitch went from Maya Angelou to Martha Stewart in a span of two months. But how was I going to tell one of my dearest friends that she was having an identity crisis?

"Molly girl you in danger," is how I opened up the conversation as we sat in the nail shop waiting for our gels to dry. (Yes, I know a bit dramatic, but what do you expect from a drama queen.) She looked into my eyes with this blank stare and then started airing all of her concerns about her still, new relationship and the thought that her prince charming maybe roaming.

My mother was right. (I hate it when she's right.) Nikita had gotten caught in a vicious cycle a lot of Blacks get caught in. It's called the do I need to be Whiter to please?" Syndrome. You take a very strong independent Black person and have them fall in love with a White man/woman and in all the pictures on their wall began to magically become full of White people. So much so that you find yourself asking do you know any Black people?

Nikita had not gotten that far but she had allowed her relationship with a White man who "acted" Black to turn her into a Black woman who "acted" White. I told her what my mother said and at first, she laughed it off, but I could tell that what I had told her did get to her.

Nikita went home that day and took a good look at herself in the mirror. It was at that moment that she realized that somewhere along the way, she had lost her true Black self. Nikita's situation had me thinking damn should I try some White/Black dick so I could be brainwashed? This might deserve some investigation. I came up with a solid "NO."

I know that a lot of you are saying "I have never and would not ever." But until you are face to face with a situation you have no idea how you may respond. In many cases the heart will do anything to fill the gaping womb of heartbreak or loneliness.

We all like to think we are "bad bitches" when it comes to love and "Fuck that nigga," but the truth is we are all one dick away from a bad decision. Do you know how many women are sitting behind bars for loyalty to a man? (He out being un-loyal to another woman and yo stupid ass writing pen pal letters from maximum security at Rikers.)

Nakita and her White prince charming ended up breaking up and going along their own separate paths. Nakita was devastated and went back to hating White people again. This time it was different though, she wasn't as committed as she was the last time. This time she was willing to work with them, but she still didn't trust them.

One day Nakita and I were walking through the dog park with her new puppy that I hated. The little ugly Chihuahua barked at everything. I'm not a pet fan, especially not that kind of pet fan. I know that I have lost a couple of you, but I don't care pets aren't for everybody. Anyway, we were walking, and I asked her, "did she miss Corey?," she stopped and said, "yes." That was it, that was all, and we didn't talk about it again.

By some weird twist of fate Nakita and Cory reconnected, Him a little clearer to her about what he needed from her and her a lot clearer about who she was. Me Still single as a dirty ass dollar bill. Such is my fate. There is a different glow about her now, the glow of a woman who has met the man she was meant to be with.

To be honest with you, for the most part people are on this earth searching for love. Society tells us what love should be and look like. The truth is just like when you are going to die, you never know what God has instore for you. The love of your life may not come in the package that you think it should.

My prince charming may or may not be Jon B, that fine ass Italian boy @3o1Josiah from TikTok or Tom Holland that little Flexible British White boy could get it, I'm sorry, but he can. Then again it might be so, the next time some big, tall sexy White Blackish guy comes walking towards your "Black Lives Matter's fine ass, just make sure you keep that proud fist high in the sky and I think you'll be fine.

Chapter 5

Suck dat DICK!!!

"All meat don't taste like chicken. Some of it tastes like DICK."

Gregory D. Alexander

*M*y mother always told me that "What you ain't doing somebody else will.," and I took that to heart. Did you know that when most men cheat it usually starts with the one thing that you refuse to do?, Suck a dick. Some of you prudish bitches are saying "Ewe, that's nasty. Well, this chapter is dedicated to the beautiful art of sucking a good dick. In this chapter I will be giving you tips and tricks to make it more enjoyable for you and your partner, and you again.

A hard dick is mandatory for good sex with a man, don't argue it just is. For most men in order to give you the piping your pussy deserves, it's going to need a little inspiration. You have to get the dick it peak potential in order to enjoy all its hidden talents, treasures, and explosive delights. (I know a lot about exploding penis's.)

Did you know that the same material that is on the inside of your vagina is inside your mouth? This means that you have a fully controllable pussy right in your head. All the things that you wish your untrained pussy could do with a dick you can make your well-trained mouth do with more control.

69

I started at a very young age training my throat muscles to completely envelope a dick and induce full nut showers. I'm Porno Freaky (Side note this book is not a judgment, it's about truth. If you can't handle what you're reading, that is the reason why you should continue to read.)

Here is a secret, sorry men. Most men would be content with just some head every day. With the stresses of the day, it's really all a man wants. The feeling of your dick in a warm mouth and releasing the contents of your sac is all they really need. To most men all you have to do is call and say, "When you get home, I'm 'ma suck the color off your dick." I bet he will not make a stop.

As hard as we try to make them complex about everything, men are pretty simple about sex. Good head, good pussy every now and again they will be fine. I say this to say that it's not that men don't cheat, because some do, it's just that for the most part, it's not as cerebral as women.

Men will cheat just because they keep asking you to suck they dick and you keep saying "No!," It's just that simple. You running around telling your friends, "I gave him everything he wanted.," really, did you? Yes ladies it's that simple stop thinking so hard, what I said is what I said. It doesn't have to be some big reason and you being a bad wife, girlfriend, or boyfriend, no they just wanted some head, and you were too proud to choke on it.

I know that it's very hard for you to understand that the ending of your relationship came down to you not giving that sloppy toppy. The truth is in a lot of cases, it did. He asked, you said no, he went and got it, you found out cause men are sloppy, and you left him, the end.

Ladies, men don't just stop wanting something because you said no. When you ask him to get your nails did and he said no, did that stop you from wanting them done? Somebody just said "No, I just go and get them done myself." Yes, any human being should. Some of you missed the connection. You just said, "that's not the same." YES IT IS! It is what they want. What makes you think that wants aren't as important to some people as needs are to others? And furthermore, who are you to tell someone whether something is a want or a need? (That's why you single, bitch)

I have rarely in my life met a man that didn't like head. I have met more men that didn't like intercourse than I have men that don't like head. Most men who tell you they don't like head just don't like the way you do it. They would rather not get a half ass blow job.

71

Some of you are asking "How do I know if I'm giving a half ass blow job?" It's simple, you've come to the right place. If he tells you to stop, he doesn't grab your head or moan," you fucking up. Men may not be very vocal about a lot of things when it comes to their feelings, but when it comes to "Head," they will tell you what the last girl did to make it feel good in order to get you on the right path. You just have to listen.

Why is it that women claim to be such great communicators, but don't listen? When it comes to finding out about what a man likes, they would rather go deaf, blind, and dumb. The fear of hearing something so far out there just paralyzes them. Not every man is going to tell you he likes a finger up his ass. You are more worried about his masculinity than he is. (Some do like a lil prostate massage. Just letting you know.)

Ladies he wants to wiggle and moan just like you. I can assure you there is nothing better sexually than to see than a man almost going into convulsions from nutting so hard. I dated this guy from Belize once that yelled when he nutted. That shit used to drive me wild. It also helped that his dick was big as hell, and he was fine as hell.

His reaction to nutting turned me on so much that it was my goal to get him to climax as much as I could. I craved to hear that sound. It was how I knew that I had spent him. Yes, that's right I had drained him dry and made him smile every night before he went to sleep. I was obsessed with sucking his dick.

I was so obsessed that I would dream about it when we were not together. I am more about his pleasure than mine when it comes to sex. Now don't get me wrong, I need to get where I'm going too. But for the most part when you are with the right person, if you are doing them a solid, they will do you one. The law of reciprocity.

We hear a lot about these relationships that end because the partners stopped touching each other. I'm not going to tell you that sucking your man's dick every night is going to keep him. Let me ask you a question though, when have you ever heard a man say, "I broke up with them because they suck my dick every night?" That statement has never been uttered on any day of any man's life in history. Men may not want to have sex every day, but when given the opportunity to lay back do nothing as you bring them to orgasm, they are always down.

I have this older friend, whom we will call Marjorie, Marjorie is a woman of a certain age with certain values and standards and so she dates accordingly. I can talk to Marjorie about a lot of things when it comes to me, but she is very secretive when it comes to her exploits, which truthfully I understand.

Marjorie went on this dating site for older Black women and met Joe. Joe used to own a funeral parlor, he had sold his business and retired. Joe was not your average old man and really didn't need the site to find a woman, (He was fine for 60) Joe was in shape with a full head of hair chocolate skin, and a beautiful white smile, which would make even the hardest thug smile back in passing.

After over 30 years with his wife, Joe had had enough of not being pleased. He had given his life faithfully and did not want to spend the rest of his life not getting what he wanted. Joe posted on his profile this list of things he was looking for in a woman. Let's just say obviously Marjorie was blinded by the smile.

Joe liked to eat pussy, ass and get his dick sucked, and as blunt as it sounds, it's exactly how he wrote it. When Marjorie showed me his freaky-ass profile, it was the first thing that I noticed. "Marjorie.," I said then continued. "Girl, you know this man like a Lil sloppy toppy with his coffee in the morning?" Marjorie was oblivious to what I was talking about. "Girl, he likes to get head, get his dick sucked.." The

74

look on Marjorie's 57-year-old face was that of confusion. At that point, I realized that she had never placed her lips upon a man's happy place in her life. Marjorie was from an age when women did not talk about or do such things.

A lot of you new-age boys and girls may not believe it but not so long ago there was a time when being sexually adventurous was very much frowned upon. Yes, there was a day when we had to pretend like we didn't like a little "Starburst" in our mouths.

I said, "Gurl, now you know you gon have to suck this man's dick right?" Marjorie metaphorically clutched her pearls so hard that she snatched them from her neck. I had never in my life seen someone so appalled at the thought. I mean I had been putting dicks in my mouth willingly since I was about 15. (Remember what I said about being honest.) Sucking dick was just a part of the show.

Right at that moment Marjorie and 100's of years of her foremothers scoffing at the thought of orally pleasing their man, stood up and walked out of the room. I wasn't surprised, I did however wonder how I ended up with such a prude as a friend? It was just a little dick.

Marjorie called me that night and apologized for abandoning me. She then asked what she should do. She really liked this man. I told her she should buy some knee pads (No I didn't) But I did advise her that she and her 57-year-old pussy was not magical enough to make this man forget that at some point he was going to want some head. If she was going to go any further, she needed to suck him off.

As crass as the saying "Suck him off" sounds, that's just what it is. Open your mouth and your throat and suck it until his toes curl. Lubricate your throat and make it do what it do.

After two months of dating, Marjorie and Joe became sexual and the conversation of oral sex was broached. I had given Marjorie some of my secrets to success and she was ready, that is, until the next day. Marjorie told me "He pulled out that ugly thing and I stared at it for a minute and decided Nah, no need in changing who I am now."

I was proud of Marjorie for sticking to her values, however misguided I thought they were. I do believe that you should never be forced to do something sexually that you don't want to do. But don't be mad when there is another somebody out there that is willing to do what you won't. Marjorie is still single and has yet to put another dick in her mouth.

Marjorie is still on the dating site, this time she is a little more careful about who she connects with. If I were to be honest, I think that the decision she made was stupid, a well off, handsome older man that looked that good and could still fuck, I would have sucked his dick until rigor mortis set in. It is hard to find a "worth it" man out here in these streets.

Yeah, yeah, yeah, I know. You are dying to know the secret to sucking a good dick. These skills that I am about to teach you have been passed down from the ancient gays on to me. You need to be grateful that I am about to tell you the gay man's secret to sucking a dick better than a woman.

1. When you start you have to look him dead in the eye like you are about to go to work. Pucker your lips and tap the dick on them all while looking at him. (side note dry lips mean dry ass head and ain't nobody got time for that. Moisten them lips.)

2. Take your tongue and lick from the bottom of the shaft to the tip while at the tip test the sensitivity of the head by just wrapping

your lips around it. If any jumping or jerking activity occurs in the man note that. There are nerve endings there. "Head" is supposed to be a completely pleasurable experience.

Some men have overly sensitive heads and any direct attention to the head will take them out of the moment. Men are usually very vocal about this. The very moment it happens they will say "My head is really sensitive, believe them. When this happens don't get scared. It just means don't make the head your objective. The shaft is what you should focus on. In this case, Deep throating would have to be more frequently, still not constant.

      3.   No Dry "Head." "Head" is supposed to be sloppy. No man is going to say to you "Give me some of your dry head." If they do girl, you're doing something wrong, and I can't help you. Make it wet. Remember what I said earlier about your mouth being a pussy you have complete control over. (The extra added bonus is you also have a tongue there.

      4.   Most men want you to swallow. You might think it's gross, but it is what it is. The second option is on your face which is kind of pornish, but it gets the job done. Men want to know that their seed is either deep inside you or all over you. (Side note, no man wants to see you spit their nut out. They don't say anything

about it, but they do notice it. Let it dribble out of your mouth. It's the best of both worlds for them.

5. Lastly, this is the biggest secret of them all. Enjoy it. If you enjoy it, they will. The more you enjoy it the more you are open to suggestions and listening. Men will moan when it feels good, and for those that don't moan, they will tell you in body movement when you are getting the job done.

Some of you are saying right now that it's all just nasty, But I'm sure by now you know that this book is a little nasty. If no one ever talks about the nasty stuff, how will you know how to handle it? For God's sake people, it's just sucking a damn dick you put a whole damn dead animal carcass down your throat almost every day, what's a live pulsating dick?

Chapter 6

Oh, the family.

"His mom was calling me a nigger in Spanish and didn't think I knew it, Bitch. She lucky her son had good dick."

Gregory D. Alexander

*F*amily, La Familia, Famille, or however you say it can be a pain in your left ass cheek, especially mother's. Many women will tell you stories of how they do not get along with their mothers-in-law. They generally start with "This bitch." As much as you try to respect them, they have a problem with you. Don't worry they are preprogrammed to be this way.

I wanna get this out of the way first. I am not about to tell you that there is some creepy "she wants to be the one he is sleeping with story, because for the most part that is not the case. Please stop using that as your issue with his mother. At that point, you are just grasping at straws that don't exist. (IT'S HIS MOTHER, BITCH!!!) I don't give a fuck who you are to him. If he values anybody above his "Good" mother, or daughter throw him back in the ocean. Yes, you heard it here.

A man who value's his mother will value you. You are the problem. I know you're like, "Well, I haven't done anything, "Yes you have." I'll explain. In the mind of a man

81

who has been loved correctly by his mother, you will never mean more to him than her. Your pride is stopping you from realizing that. Instead of working against the natural order of things, you and she should be working together. That way you both can get what you want.

"What are you talking about Greg?" She had him, she has been his queen since birth. You are his wife/girl-friend/jump-off something that is replaceable. His mother ain't going nowhere. He will love her before, during and after you. I assure you; you do not want to be with a man that you helped to create a wedge between him and his mother. No matter how wrong he may know she is. It is still his mother. You have been outwitted from the moment of conception.

I know it sounds good when you hear books and Tyler Perry tell you how things should be. But baby if things were how they should be we would still not be happy. Nobody starts a sentence with "I wasn't doing what I should be doing, and he still left me. I don't know what I was doing wrong." People have the need to have a victim and a villain in their story. If you are constantly making his mother, the villain in your story it won't end well.

I'll take my mother for example. There is no one in the world that loves me more than my mother. Through the tears, revelations, and bad decision she has told me "You act like you ain't got nowhere to go. Bring yo ass home."

There are a lot of things in this world that are not forever but for most of us a mother's love is one thing that we can always count on. It was her decision to bring you into the world, to let you occupy space in her body to hold you, heal you and make sure that you didn't die along the way. My respect for my mother is endless. Don't get me wrong, she gets on my nerves sometimes, but you will never mean to me what my mother means to me. Not sorry, no apologies and no need for you to have hurt feelings. It is what it is. Unbelievably though they may not say it, most men feel this way.

I have a friend, Nancy. Nancy was at a speakeasy when she met Christopher. He was a well-dressed white man with the most seaworthy blue eyes she had ever seen in her life. (Her description, not mine, they were just blue to me.) After dating for 6 months Christopher decided that it was time to introduce Nancy to his family. Nancy had thought that she was making a good impression until one day she had decided to volunteer to take his mother grocery shopping. Nancy knew that she had a hair appointment, but she thought that it would allow her to get closer and she could still make it to the appointment.

(Here's where I interject, she was trying too hard.)

Upon meeting Nancy, Christopher's mother had already sized her up and determined how she was going to break Nancy down. Nancy had no idea that she was just a pawn in the sick and twisted game that was in front of her. She thought that she was going to do something nice. What she didn't know was that she was now in the biggest test of her patients that she would ever experience.

Christopher's mother had been a pro at this sort of thing. The moment she got into the car Christopher's mother Pam complained about the air setting saying that it was too cold. Nancy adjusted the air 5 times before Pam was content, no not happy, but content. Let's keep in mind, Nancy is not a patient person at all. When they got to the grocery story Nancy knew that she only had a certain amount of time to spend on this "nice thing" that she was doing. Pam had to go down every aisle and look at the back of every label.

Pam noticed the frequency that Nancy looked at her fit bit and then asked, "am I holding you from something?" not wanting to seem like she was rushing, Nancy lied, and said, "not at all." Pam knew then that she had Nancy in the palm of her hands. She decided that she was going to take

an even longer time. This caused Nancy to miss her appointment. Nancy was furious as she sat next to Pam driving her
home.

Pam wasn't through yet though. Pam had decided
that this would be the perfect time to tell Nancy that she
could not drive in a not-so-subtle passive-aggressive way
"Oh baby, you missed that stop sign but that's okay, I'm still
alive I guess it wasn't that important." Where you get your
license?" and "My God, We got here so fast I don't remember leaving the parking lot."

When they reached the house, Nancy all but pushed
her future mother-in-law out of her car and drove off. She
left so fast that there were groceries still in the back seat.
That night Nancy told Christopher about how his mother
had monopolized her whole day and how she had offended
her. He attempted to be supportive, said he was sorry and
moved on to another topic. Nancy was secretly so offended
by this.

The next day when Nancy brought this up in our
friend's group I asked her, "What did she expect him to
do?" She started her sentence with "He should tell her" and
I stopped her immediately. "He should not tell her anything.
What happened had nothing to do with him. Why is he get-

ting involved." She said, "You're a man you don't understand." I said, "You're a woman you will never understand." Well let's just say that didn't go over so well in a group of women. Ladies, being a woman does not make you right about everything just because you feel some kind of way, (Yeah, I said it.)

The person that you have an issue with is his mother. The person that you are creating a problem with is him. You won't win this. First off, most men don't get involved in women's issues and they most definitely ain't about to check their mother. Especially just because you are too prideful to know that sometimes you must go along to get along.

I'm going to let you in on a little secret. The moment he agreed to let you do something alone with his mother they already talked about it. She already told him that she was going to fuck with you. He told her to "take it easy" but she said "If you gon marry this one, I need to know what kind of woman she is. I might have to live with y'all when I get old."

Did you notice how I rushed to marriage? If someone introduces you to their family in most cases the conversation of marriage has come up. A mother does not want someone in their family that they don't wanna see over the holidays. Nancy had already told Pam that she was not the one for her son by how she handled the situation.

First, rather than just asking Pam what air setting she preferred and allowing her to make that decision, she showed Pam that it was hard for her to release control.

Second Nancy stood to the side during the grocery trip checking her watch and not engaging in the moment. This showed she wasn't flexible or patient and that she only did what she was doing for the optics.

Third, when Nancy was asked had she had something to do, she lied. Prior to the trip Christopher had already asked that his mother didn't take too long because Nancy had something to do. That meant she wasn't honest.

Fourth on the trip home she was so visually irritated by the critiques of her driving she left Christopher's mother on the curb quite frankly "holding the bag." When the going gets tough she gets going.

When Pam got to talk to her son, she talked about how Nancy had reacted, and Christopher, having had already heard the story knew what he had to do. The next day he broke up with Nancy. Why would he marry a woman who could not be herself without motive, tell the truth, be flexible, patient, and would cut and run when the going gets tough?

I know you're saying, "She didn't know she was getting tested." That is the point. Your Character is what it is. Pam's behavior was a direct reflection of her son. She knows the things that Nancy would have to put up with to be an effective partner for her son. In a way, she actually saved Nancy from heartache.

Nancy didn't see it that way and the defiant woman in you doesn't either. Turns out a side friend of mine is dating Christopher now and the very behavior that his mother displayed is the very thing that she complains to me about him. The difference is she knew how to play the game.

Christophers mother knows all the secrets to get what she wanted from Christopher and because she likes this side friend of mines, she shared the secrets. The mother knows best. Remember what I said about working together? When you choose to step out of your own way and stop standing on your ego you will be blessed with wisdom. (Or you can just read this book.)

We have been told by so many people and so many things that life is supposed to be perfect, but it's not. Mothers protect their sons. When you have one you will be the same way. You won't want your son to marry some two-bit, angry floozy he met off a corner.

Ladies stop fighting against the grain about everything. All relationships look different. Yes, we all want to be respected for our position in any situation. The truth is in all situations you won't be. You must learn that some battles just aren't worth fighting. Now don't just let the battle axe all out disrespect you and if he is a good man, he won't let her either, but stop trying to be the Queen Elizabeth when you are only a Camilla Parker Bowles, you'll get your time.

So, when it is that you encounter the mother-in-law from hell, practice patience and understanding and watch those facial expressions. You just might be getting tested.

Chapter

7

I got a friend in me.

"The best nut I have ever had, happened when nobody else was around."

Gregory D Alexander

*S*o, I have a friend we'll call Anna. She said to me one-day "baby, what I need a man for?" We were having a very in-depth conversation about self-care. (Wink, wink) She went on to tell me about her special friend. I laughed but, on the inside, I was deeply troubled.

92% of men and 76% of women in the United States masturbate. That brings the world total of people who choke the chicken, spank the monkey, play in their carpet, jerk, jack, and wank themselves to a whopping 76%. (Bet you think about that the next time someone comes and shakes your hand.)

A once so taboo thing that's a part of popular culture is still a taboo thing apart of taboo culture. People wake up, get home from work, at work before they go to bed want a release. This says more about the world we live in than how nasty you may think the activity might be.

Now I don't know the science behind it. I do know however that a good morning nut relieves tension and allows me to at least for a few minutes in my day have a clear mind. The thought of not nutting in a day is just plain dreadful. I'm not into punishment. Yes, I am like the other 76% of adults in the world who masturbate. Why might you ask?

91

Bitch, it feels good. And just like you have experienced in your bedroom. Most men just don't know how to finish the job they started. (I can see the men getting angry.) Most bottoms and women of the world know exactly what I'm talking about. You get in the bed; he gets his nut, and you like "well where's mine?"

(Side note: Here's a tip. You want to piss him off, and make him try harder to get you where you need to go? When he gets done, pull out your dildo. (It must be bigger than his dick to work.) Fuck yourself like you are one of those porno girls. I mean moan and drool put on a show and enjoy it. Sometimes you must kill a man's ego in order to get him to act right. If this doesn't work throw him away and start over, he ain't even trying, he's trash.) You have the permission you need to be pleased. Sex is not just for reproduction. We do it because it feels good too. But I'm getting off-topic.

For the 24% of people in the world that don't nut daily, please tell me how you make it through life. People, places, and things are just too stressful. God created the orgasm for two purposes, one to procreate and two because you just need to feel good. I dare any of you to name one thing that feels better than getting a good nut. At the thought of it, some of you'll are twiddling your lips now. It's ok you have my permission go get one now, I'll wait. Mr. Feel good is in your nightstand.

With the explosion of sites like Twitter, tumbler Pornhub and Hamster getting access to seeing your former Highschool prom king and queen bare it all and bust a nut right in front of you. (I was born in the wrong age of technology.) I would have died to see my high school crush on Twitter giving me a show I would never forget. My point is these sites provide more proof that just about everybody is getting a good nut but you. And if you are getting a good nut there's no need to be ashamed of it.

The best nuts I have ever had have all been by the hands of, well, me. No pun intended. It's usually some new thing that I have found on Pornhub that I didn't know I was interested in until I saw it. Forrest Gump said it best, "Life is like a box of chocolates, you never know what your gon get." Well in this case it's like an internet search for Big Dick, you never know what might pop up. I found out that I'm into men fucking toys. There's something about seeing the reckless abandon of this big Black dick fucking this toy that just takes me to another planet. I don't know what it is about it, but the shit is hot.

Everybody has their kink. Whatever yours is, I hope you have found it and it gets you where you need to go. Too many of you are walking around not knowing how to please yourself which make you the wrong person to tell someone else how to please you. Some things feel good every now and again, not always. Wouldn't you like to know what the thing is that gets you there all the time? You won't know if you never explored.

Now that all that's been said, let's get back to my friend Anna. Anna is a very high-priced attorney for a firm in New York. With Bosses clients and brief's her day is as she puts it a "Fucking Shit Show" every day. Anna has been single since her fiancé was caught getting his dick sucked by a bottle service girl he met at a super bowl party. (Dick sucking is something Anna refuses to do by the way.)

Anna started getting random text from a mysterious number. Just "hey babe." It wasn't from her fiancé, so she didn't pay it any mind, maybe they had the wrong number. The person's text weren't eliciting a response, so they decided to use his name. Somehow the tramp had gotten Anna's number and decided that she was going to out Anna's fiancé. (Just FYI most men are caught because they are not smart enough to keep their personal life out of the transaction. Women cheat better.)

After this had happen Anna confronted her cheating man and told him the wedding was off. Anna had been through this before and at that point, decided that she was going to not date men. She wasn't interested in changing sides, so she had to look for an alternative. Anna happened upon "The Rose," A clitoris stimulator she had found online, and since then she has become addicted to it.

The Rose is a motorized "Coochie Monster" that has become all the rage with single, sexually frustrated with men, women. My friend Anna was on the ground floor with this thing. The way she raved about it, you would think that she had stock in the thing. Knowing her she probably does.

When she first mentioned it at the table all the girls scoffed at the thought. Little did I know all of them had it on backorder. After just a couple of weeks, the conversation at the table was a little lighter. There was less talk about men and more about things like art, hair, stock, and the economy. Okay, I'm lying all these heffa's ever wanted to talk about was how much this little rose thing that looked like a coffee table air freshener had changed their lives. I got worried for men everywhere.

Listen if this thing takes over the world how will you heffa's and those assholes out there ever procreate to make more of Me's? I'm tired of the dreadful ones that are walking around now. We need a new batch. The "Gremlins" have run amuck. I'm not going to go in completely on this generation but bitch, some of you need to be a little more selective about who it is you procreating with. This batch of twenty somethings ain't worth the condoms you forgot to put on.

Okay maybe I'm being a little harsh. Not all the twenty something's are trash. But hell, we get to see how trashy most of them are on TicTok, whereas in my generation we didn't have all these apps that would have exposed us. Truthfully, my generation was no better, but you have no proof, but I digress. Back to your originally scheduled program.

I didn't know where to go from here until a lightbulb went off. I was having a conversation with one of my straight male friends Dre. Dre is a very attractive yoga instructor I met while I was pretending to be working out at the gym. He asked me what I was doing Friday night. I thought he was asking me on a date. He was actually asking me to join his class. I didn't join, but I did get a good friend out of it.

All of my friends want me to hook them up with him but, sorry girl's I know too much about you heffa's to ruin this man's life like that. (Lol) I don't know why it is that you all don't think that while we are sitting and talking with you, that we ain't keeping notes. (Some of you girls is just nasty.)

Dre is a man's man. He's into sports, beers, his body, and getting girls. With him being so good-looking the getting girls part is not that hard for him. I said to Dre one day, already assuming that he masturbates (96% of men in America, remember?) "Do you use toys when you mastur- bate?" I could tell that initially, the question made him un- comfortable but then Dre answered with something surpris- ing. "Yeah, I have a pocket pussy."

I don't know why but the moment the word's pocket pussy fell from his lips, there was a glow in him I had never seen before. It was like he had grown some sort of at- tachment to the thing. It was a manlier exact feeling of what I experienced with Anna and the girls. His spirit lit up, the edges of his mouth turned upwards, and tone changed to that of a child on Christmas day.

The way that he described this thing was "It's like a headless torso of a woman it has breast a vagina and an ass- hole, all of which he professed to make good use of. I then asked, "Why a pocket pussy when you have all these girls ready and willing?," he answered, "Because, I'm also a

97

man," his answer didn't shock me. "They don't complain, I do what I want. I bust a nut and then go about my day. Women want you to do this, and that and can't take dick the way I like to give it. Sometimes I just want to throw dick and not wait, not slow down, not speed up, just fuck bust my nut throw the pussy on the floor and go to sleep."

What Dre was telling me in short was that his toy was just a way for him to release without commitment or restraint. He didn't see it as a replacement, it was just a convenience, a convenience he thoroughly enjoyed but a convenience, nonetheless.

Anna had a toy of necessity to feel good and replace something that was missing. What would the world be like if people like Dre and Anna could openly have this conversation with each other? Would it improve their sex lives?

After a while Anna had become numb to natural stimuli Dre's dick could never perform the sucking and vibrating of the magical "The Rose." Try as she might Anna would never allow Dre to do whatever he wanted to do to her. (She has control issues.) This means that masturbation is and will always be a necessity for her. Everybody, but you is doing it. (Yes, I'm calling you out.)

Boom did I drop the bomb? Did I tell the big secret? I would look weird at those who don't do it. I would wonder things like, "How many bodies are in your front yard? and "How bad is your road rage?" Sexually repressed people make other people's lives a living hell. They walk around with sour puss faces dealing out there frustrations to the undeserving of us. We don't want it. Comprende?

When going out into this new dating landscape, don't be afraid to ask questions about masturbation and toys. You might come across something interesting you want to try. Stop making pleasure your taboo. You know that saying, "If everybody's jumping off a bridge are you going to jump?" in this case the answer is yes. So go twiddle your fingers in that dry ass pussy and bring it back to life. 76% of your sisters in the struggle are already doing it.

Chapter 8

You're having his spawn.

"Children make me want to get a vasectomy."

Gregory D. Alexander

*W*omen feel trapped too. I know that sounds terrible, but this book is about "The Truth of Love, Life, and Sex. (Hell, it's the name of the book.) I will always tell the truth and the truth is not every woman wants to have your baby. Sometimes they were just drunk and didn't have enough money to "Plan B" the shit out of your future demon spawn growing inside of them.

I am not here to judge, okay well I'm a little judgy but for me, children are an inconvenience, something I have to think about before I consider my own needs. This is just one of the reasons why I don't have any now. I mean other than the fact that I'm gayer than a peacock sitting on top of a sequined covered piano while Liberace is playing Abba's "Dancing Queen." As you can tell I am not a fan of children or animals so who better to tell you about the fruits of not having them than me?

Long, long ago people set out into the world attempting to build things and tend fields, this is long before that pesky little thing called slavery happened. People figured they couldn't do it all by themselves. It was too hard. One day a woman opened her legs and a whole workable human just popped out. Men knew at that point that they had it all figured out. They had their help.

Suddenly, this Boom happened. People were having 20 odd in one family. The kids were just dropping out of vaginas at church. (Gives new meaning to Oh Lord, right?) Finally, the labor shortage crisis was cured. Fast forward thousands of years later and we don't need kids for those purposes anymore. Now you have kids either because you want them, or you were too horny to put on a condom.

With the price of everything and the lack of space in the world, people are not having kids at the rate that they were in the early hundreds. Women are realizing more that they don't need to have sex just for reproductive purposes and require all parties involved to protect themselves from having an unplanned pregnancy or a reason to get an abortion.

Abortion, I know that word just has your knickers in a bunch. Yeah, I'm going to talk about it. There have been many times I have been waiting in the car for a friend or family member who has had to make the ultimate decision to end a life. The tears and uneasiness that come over them consume them because they have made a mistake. They now have to make a decision that they never thought that they would have to make. Oh yes, Though I know not the pain of it I know the emotional toll it can take.

I think of the many kids I would have had if I were a female and think, God knew not to make this hoe a female. You get caught up in the moment. It's not like you plan to do it, it just happens. You know most will tell you "No you stop and say put a condom on.," but I know the truth. The truth is that you get caught in the moment and the last thing on your mind is "where is my condoms?." With the disparity of marriage and actual full-blown relationships in this day and most pregnancies happen between two people who don't know each other.

A friend of mine, I'll call her Maria, met a guy at an industry social. They hit it off from the start. He was just the kind of guy she liked to fuck. After about 4 drinks each, Maria and the guy were feeling a Lil "randy" if you know what I mean. They went back to her place and about two missed periods later Maria was pregnant. She didn't even know the man's name, well she knew it, but she was drunk so now she didn't remember it.

Maria had no plans on having kids and this was not going to be the time that she had a change of heart. She had just booked this new series and hadn't worked in ages. She needed this gig like a crackhead needs a crack. When she told me she was pregnant I was a little surprised. She's that one friend that we all have that loathes the thought of having kids. When it comes to passing out condoms, she'd be the purse you dive into.

Maria asked me to go with her to get this abortion, and I was more than happy to. This was not my first ride at the Rodeo. While we drove there, I asked the questions anybody you use as your accomplice would. "Did you try to find the father and are you sure you want to do this" Choosing to end a life can have terrible ripple effects on your future. Making this decision can change your life.

She had not tried to find the father, and, she was sure. I couldn't tell by the way her tears were soaking through my newly detailed car seats. As we pulled up to the place I asked again, "Are you sure you want to do this?" She looked at me with red puffy eyes and said, "I don't have a choice."

I don't know why those words particularly hit me the most. Maybe because they seemed so hopeless. I'm sure that many women have been in this position before. Standing at the doors between, their life and creating one and wondering which one to go through. Though she was not doubting which door to go through, she was doubting whether what she was doing would be the right thing.

As a man, I'm not here to tell you what to do with your body at all. How can I? I have never had to face whatever it is that you must face and try to figure out how to move around. I most definitely would have been pregnant multiple times if I were a woman. So, telling you what's right would most likely end in me telling myself to "Shut the fuck up. This ain't your struggle." So, all you people who are judging right now. I am not taking a stand for anything but my own business. I will support my friends no matter what I might think about their decisions.

When I and Maria left the building, I could tell that she was deeply troubled by her decision. We rode to her house in silence and never talked about that day again. Two months later after getting the role on the show, an extra reporter asked her if she ever wanted to have kids and for a second there she looked into the camera with a blank stare and then caught herself and said, "one day." I could tell that she was thinking about the moment not two months ago.

I was sad for Maria, and I wanted to hug her. I knew she needed it right at that moment. The next time I saw her. I looked at her, she looked at me, and it was like we both knew exactly what each other was thinking. But as I said before we never talked about it again.

Having a baby was not the right decision for her at that moment. But here's another thing that bothers me though. I have never seen an interview where a man was asked whether he wanted to have kids. Why was it imperative that the reporter ask Maria that question?

Women are expected to have children. As idiotic as it sounds because by nature women are the bearers of children. The world expects that they will, should, and must have children. Even when having a child is in no way what they want. This is one of those cases where I have to point out that, yes it seems outdated that we have this thought as a society, but that doesn't change the fact that it is the thought.

I close my eyes sometimes and think about how different my life would be if I had decided that children were the right path for me. I would still be stuck in Detroit because I am in no way a deadbeat but knowing what I know about myself in my reality. I would be miserable. Yeah, I hear you "yea for kids!!!" people out there. But kids are not the path for everybody. Where you see "kids being kids, and little tyke's" I see a loud, sticky, needy little crumb snatcher stealing my life force. I'm not willing to lose my soul just yet. Neither are a lot of other people in the world.

I dare you to think about the different life decisions you would have made if you didn't have them. I'm not saying regret that you did, I'm saying see the world from another point of view. One that is not your own.

When sitting down to write this chapter I thought about all the possible ways that my opinion might turn readers off because the "baby gang" is strong. I realized however that it is my truth and even though you breeders out there think that children are the "Know all be all" I humbly disagree.

People should in no way feel forced to have children. There is a caveat, however. You must be honest about how you feel. DO NOT get in a relationship with someone who wants kids in hopes that one day you or they will change their minds about how they feel about it. Don't set yourself up.

It's a very rare occasion that you will meet someone who wants children that will say "Hey, I change my mind. I don't want them" and, really mean it. There will come that one day when their siblings will bring their new bundle of terror around and all these maternal or paternal feelings will rush over them, and you will have the world's most awkwardly uncomfortable car ride on the way back home. (Those that have been in that car just silently say, "Yeah.")

I'm not saying that the first thing you should say to someone is you don't want kids. What I am saying is maybe about the second or third date you should be making it known. After that, your window is coming to a close to get out and run for the hills. I'm sure some beautiful, gay man dreaming of a family with me is reading this and saying, "I don't want him." I'm saying thank you, all the heavy lifting is done.

For all you people over 35 out there that have passed the age of wanting to create new life. I have not forgotten you. At 35 by the time that child becomes eighteen you will be well in your fifties. Do you really want to be a doting parent in your 50's? I'll be the first to say it "Baby your ship has sailed." I mean if you want to have kids at that point, have at it. Just know that the 35-year-old body ain't a 20-year-old body and it's not just a pregnancy it's a "Geriatric Pregnancy".

"Geriatric" is the biggest turn-off EVER! That word just implies that you are old as hell. In laymen's terms "you are too old to be fucking all willy nilly; do you realize what this might do to you?" I'm not making this shit up, that's what the shit really means. I mean I added some color to it. But tell me I'm wrong.

I think the term was created to detour older women from having babies. "If we scare them, they may stop this nearly impossible feat. Women have been known to have children well into their 50s. (This is another case of just because you can, should you really?)

I'm sure you know where I stand on having children at this point. But you, if you want to have them, go right ahead. That's none of my business. All that I ask is you pay others the same respect. Just because it's the decision that you decided to make, don't try to make your decisions someone else's responsibilities. Now go forth be fruitful and multiply, or not, it's up to you.

Chapter 9

You, me +

"If it's your friend I met yesterday, I might think about it."

Gregory D. Alexander

*A*HHH, the threesome. History has taught us that most things are better in three's, The charmed ones, destiny's child, The Supremes, the holy trinity, and sex. Yes, that's right, an extra set of hands touching your body at the same time as another is doing other unspeakable things to you. This is some people's fantasy. As someone who has been a part of a few, I can tell you it's not for me.

Truthfully for a lot of couples, the threesome is the last-ditch effort to save their ailing sex life (Of course that doesn't apply to everyone for those who are saying, "that's not why we did it." Another terrible happenstance of a threesome is that the relationship in a lot of cases never recovers from them.

That's why I always say, whenever you choose to go down that route with your partner, don't. Threesomes are so much better when it's random. There is no emotional commitment. You're hot, he's hot, she's hot, or whatever the combination it may be, and you are drunk on the dance floor, and you all just fuck. See how "Hot" That sounds.

Random sex acts of this sort are supposed to be hot, not complicated. People are jealous, hell even animals will cut you over their boo. Women are especially territorial.

111

There may be a few but most women don't want you me or a tree anywhere near their man. Then you throw in watching another woman make him smile the way that she feels she is supposed to. Sounds to me like the ingredients for a war.

Let's take for example 75% of the fights on shows like love and hip hop are over what? A man and not because he is so good but the fact that, said man is with another woman. This woman is in their friend group some kind of way. (The producers make sure of it.)

Does the fact that you know the woman, set it up, or okayed the activity make it a better situation? It should but here on planet earth that shit doesn't matter. We say a lot of things implying that we are going with the flow and down for anything when in reality that couldn't be further from the truth. You could be right in the middle of it and feel like "if this bitch kiss my man one more time Im'ma strangle this hoe."

The complexities of the human mind as we navigate silly things like emotions. I am a proponent for not saying you won't or can't do something because you never know until you are actually in the situation. But this one is a "Girl learn from other people's folly and sit this one out."

I have a friend Marco and his husband were at a Starbucks in Hollywood when this cute barista started flirting with Marco. Marcos's husband feeling adventurous told Marco to get the guy's number. Later that night Marco and his husband invited the Barista over for drinks one thing led to another and the three found themselves entangled.

The barista must have had some magic booty because to let Marco tell it his husband was drooling all over the place and came within minutes of entry. This was something he had never done with Marco. After the session, Marcos husband was already planning the next time that they would do this again.

Needless to say, Marco was troubled. Being the bottom in the relationship he felt that it was his job to please his man in that way. By the way that his husband responded to the sex, it was apparent to him that he was not doing the job.

Marco and Harry, his husband had been together for 10 years and for both of them the sex was getting stale. Even with that in mind, Marco had never thought about inviting someone into the relationship. It was so sad as I looked at my friend and saw the actual moment that he realized that he had killed his relationship.

I know you are saying how dramatic but let me go on. Marco told his husband how uncomfortable with the situation he was. He was thinking that he had an understanding. Needless to say, there was no understanding.

Marco's husband had begun to see the barista on the low. The kicker is I'm the one that found out. I was in Paris of all places, being an international hoe, and guess who I happened upon at the Eiffel that was supposed to be on a business trip.

I battled for a week with whether I should say something about it. Keep in mind it was not my business and I preach the gospel of minding your business very often. I was perplexed and flustered; it ruined my whole trip. The whole time I was there I was just one call away from breaking my friend's heart.

I sat in the airport on my way back home and prayed that maybe I was mistaken but about a week later I was at Marcos's home and Marco asked me did I see his husband in Paris? I didn't know whether to lie or tell the truth. If this were a setup and harry Marco's husband had mentioned that he saw me, and I say I didn't I would be the liar.

I would love to tell you that I chose to mind my business, but I didn't. I spilled the beans. Marco was devastated. I was devastated for him. But in true gay fashion, I had become the enemy. This people is why I say, "mind your business."

People never see the truth when they are hurt, mad, or disappointed. I knew in the back of my mind that saying something was not going to fare well for me. I was being a good friend. Good friends in this day and age are a dime a dozen. So, people don't trust people. This friend that I thought that I had was mad at me.

Get this, the web that this man spun was a classic. "Baby while in Paris Greg hit on me. I just wanted to let you know you shouldn't trust him." Now let me tell you Harry is an attractive White man, but not one I would fuck. Let's just say I told y'all what kind of White guys I like.

Now the optics of it all seem a Lil sus but it was purely just coincidental. When it was all said and done. I had become the one that hit on his man. A man I didn't want. The kicker is he knew this. He just didn't want to admit that what he had was over.

The shenanigans didn't end until the barista confronted Marco at his job. When I found out I laughed just a little bit. I know your like, "Why did you laugh?," because I'm human and once you fuck me over, I don't care how bad your heart is broken. I was being a friend and you tried to make me out to be the whore who wanted your sorry ass man. (Sorry I went a little hard.)

My point is all this happened when they decided to introduce someone else to the party. The feeling of disappointment was compounded because Marco realized that if only when the idea was introduced, he would have said "Hell no," he would not be in the situation.

Now all that's not to say that this wouldn't have ever happened. Harry had the "capacity to cheat" in him from the get. I'll explain that in another chapter. It's just to say that it hits different when you allowed the person, he left you for in your bedroom in the first place.

So, I'll clarify.

When you are single two other random people = good fun. There is something amazing about being trapped between two bodies that are there for the sole purpose to please you. Especially when those two bodies are absolutely beautiful.

When you are single and two friends = Tricky, this can change the whole relationship. And you really don't want any two people to know how freaky you are. As friend's, things can happen, and you might find all your business all in the street.

When you are single a freaky friend and a random = could be fun depending on the friend and closeness. If that friend is someone you met on a freak thing, and they know someone who might be down this could be fun.

When you are in a relationship with your mate and a random = I wouldn't do it. It just doesn't end well for the most part. One partner is always less into it than the other. And why would anyone want their partner to feel uncomfortable with something of a sexual nature unless they just don't care?

When you're in an open relationship = nobody you know and watch out, they may be coming for your spot.

117

Only be open in another country and no exchanging numbers. Connections are problems.

When you're in a relationship and a friend = no one close to you should know your mate intimately. It will make all involved uncomfortable at some point.

To sum it all up threesomes are fun but. I honestly believe that mixing them with love can be disastrous. Before you and your partner decide that this is the road you want to go down weigh all the pros and cons first and if that doesn't work look at the list, I just gave you and follow it like your new Bible.

Through it all whatever you do be safe and not sorry. Be honest and don't be afraid to say "No, I don't want to do that." Live also in the thought that you denying something doesn't mean it won't happen but be strong enough to deal with it if it does.

Chapter

10

The capacity to cheat.

In our bed?

Gregory D. Alexander

"*He* is fine, I know he is not faithful." So unattractive people don't cheat? Only attractive people cheat, right? Looks have everything to do with whether you cheat. I have been a witness to a lot of crazy baseless statements in my life, but I think this one is the one that takes the cake. News flash "PEOPLE CHEAT."

There is always someone willing and able to throw their legs back bend over or suck a dick. If you think otherwise, I need you to wake the fuck up. The dream world you are living in does not exist.

Kingdoms, empires, and pantheons have fallen at the hands of someone being unfaithful. This is not me saying that everybody cheats, it's me saying that everyone has the "Capacity to Cheat," including you.

I used to think that cheating was a planned thing. People woke up and said, "Well this is what I'm going to do today." As I got older, I found out that in some cases it does happen like that but for the most part that is not how it happens.

The coworker flirts, you are going through something at home. They give you this false sense of security and on that weak moment when you have nowhere else to turn, you turn to them.

You're frisky when you're drunk and after a night of drinks with a friend or a random person, you find yourself riding the dick like a trained rodeo star.

You run into your high school crush in a random sparsely populated bathroom somewhere and he fucks you in a stall. (It can happen or has happened. Let me shut up.)

I think we would all like to believe that we would never fall victim to any of these examples, but the truth is shit happens. I know that some of you are saying I still wouldn't do it and that's fine. You are not the person I'm talking about. (Stop trying to make everything about you. You're here to understand the behaviors of others, stupid.)

If you are looking at your partner saying that he or she would never it will only make the moment that it happens even worse. We all want to look at our mates and say they are perfect; however, the world divorce rate is skyrocketing the most common reason is infidelity. Turns out people don't want to stay with you when they find out that you are a lying, cheating sack of shit. (Who would have thunk it?)

I mean after all your cooking and cleaning and dick sucking and having kids and working and doing everything you have been taught to do to keep a man/woman they still cheat. (No shit Sherlock, they do.)

I'll let you in on a little-known secret. Though you can't factor yourself out of the reasoning you can say I didn't force you to be dishonest. Let me explain. I wholeheartedly believe what you won't do someone else will. However, it is on the person to decide if they let the other person do what you're not doing.

I think that I have already mentioned this before and will probably mention it again. People require different things to function. The difference between men and women (And there are many) The biggest difference is that men will find a way to get what they want. Women will repress out of shame and regret. This is why women are better liars and cheaters than men.

Ladies, I'm about to tell your biggest secret. Most women who cheat, you will never find out about it. When a woman decides to take something to the vault not even

God, Jesus and the Holy Ghost have a good recollection of it.

Women cheat when they just can't take any more of not getting something. But unlike men when they do this, they have no intention of you finding out so when they say no face no case they really mean it. They are ten levels above DL. They are another town and country dick having. Women will only implode their homes when necessary.

But men, poor misguided men will cheat with your sister just cause she was the closest thing when his dick got hard. Men will cheat with your closest work friend. (Yes, that's right that bitch that smiles in your face every day bringing you cappuccinos. Talking about "Girl, we should hang out."

They can't help it; men aren't really wired for discretion. DL and discreet are only terms they use in hopes that you will not have their business in the street or to appear more masculine to gay men. Why it is that men just aren't smart enough to ask women how they do it the world will never know.

I don't think there is a woman alive that will divulge the secret anyway. These secrets have been passed down for generations and will only be told to their favorite daughters upon their deathbed. If you are an only daughter and your mother has not told these secrets to you. You were a daddy's girl, and she was way too smart for your trickery.

You won't be telling her secrets in your eulogy speech to her. News flash if your mother has not told you any of her unmentionables, she doesn't like you that much, or doesn't trust you or your reaction. So, if you want the dish, get the stick out of your ass, and loosen up.

I'm getting off-topic, this chapter is not about mothers and daughters, but, I'll get to that at a later time in another book. I have this friend we'll call him Bradford. Bradford had been married for 15 years. Bradford's co-worker Amanda was recently divorced and found herself lonely a lot.

Bradford saw the vulnerability in her and decided that he would be a friend. Bradford always had a kind word for Amanda. They started buying each other lunch. Bradford was even so bold as to refer to Amanda as his work wife to his wife Kimi.

Kimi was not insecure about it at all because Bradford had been such a good husband; attentive, kind and oh so sweet. Kimi Invited Amanda to a house party one day and asked me if I knew someone to hook her up with. Amanda seemed like a sweet girl I suggested a certain trainer friend of mine.

They did not hit it off. At the end of the night that trainer friend of mine said all she talked about was Bradford. I knew what that meant but after my incident with Marco, I have learned to mind my business. So, this time I did. (Well, kind of.) I did say to Kimi while helping with the dishes, "Amanda and Bradford are really close?" She replied, "yes." No Shade but Kimi isn't the brightest bulb on the Christmas tree.

About a month later Amanda called Bradford to come to get her from a bar she had found herself drunk in. Kimi was luxuriating in a bath and Bradford, thinking it would be a quick trip, left and picked her up to take her home. One thing led to another, and Amanda and Bradford had fucked.

When Bradford had gotten home, Kimi was asleep. He went on never mentioning he had gone. Kimi never even asked about it, well because she didn't know. Three months later Amanda is pregnant and guess who's baby it is. Kimi is devastated and asking for a divorce. She just can't believe that her perfect husband did this to her.

In an imperfect world, imperfect people do imperfect things. Why is this so hard for people to understand? We are all just one wrong decision from heartbreak. It sounds good for us to spout out things about being loyal and faithful. We have to understand that these things are decisions.

Being Loyal is a decision you have to make every time you step out the door. Some days may not be "Loyal days." That day you may not feel like it's all worth it and you don't mind risking everything that you have built.

"Oh Greg, You're wrong." "Oh, cheated on, lied to, divorced, battered, abused, and misled women. When will you learn that again nothing in life when it comes to someone else is predictable? People make different tough decisions every day.

I have learned to look at people as they are. I don't expect them to cheat or lie, I just know that they are capable of it.

"Well, Greg what should I do when it happens?." There is no perfect answer to this question. You have to weigh your pros and cons. The first one is:

Can you get over it?

This has its own implications because if you can, are you opening up the door for it to happen again?

I'm sorry no one makes a mistake and has sex with another person. They are either having it willingly or unwillingly. There is no in-between. When your Partner says I made a mistake that implies that they knew that what they were doing was a no-no. A mistake is stepping out into the street on a green light and oncoming traffic because you didn't look up. That my dear is a mistake.

The next thing to think about is are you willing to let it all go?

It's easier in this day and age to do this one because things are so expensive that more than likely both parties are employed and know the in and out of living alone unlike their mother and their mother's before them.

Lastly:

Is this worth your time?

I really hope the answer to this question is "No" But on the likely chance the answer is "Yes" (SMH) God help you poor Lil Tink, Tink.

For those of you that are expecting a finite answer. Again, there is none. You have to know your worth. Sometimes you don't think that you are worth having someone that wants only you. We don't live in a world where everybody has my level of confidence. You might think that your person is the best you will ever do or have. (I wanna say that's fine, but damn, I hate that you feel that way.)

There are so many good people out here in the world that want strong, faithful, committed situations, please find one of them. But also face the fact that all of us are not meant to be in a relationship because some of us don't know our worth. I really hope that you know yours and tell that cheating son of a bitch to take a long walk off a short peer and mean it with every grain of salt in your body.

Chapter

11

The disappointing Truth

"I could have been somebody, but then I met you. Talk about bad decisions."

Gregory Alexander

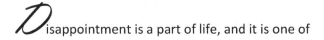isappointment is a part of life, and it is one of

the most unsuspected parts of it also. I'll explain, the reason why I say this is because you can be doing everything the way that it is supposed to be done and doing it right and still not succeed.

Disappointment can be in a person, place, or thing. Websters dictionary defines disappointment as unhappiness from the failure of something hoped for or expected to happen. When we do something, I think that we all have expectations of what the outcome will be.

I expected to be the greatest screen writer on earth by 30. Let's just say that didn't happen. Right now, somebody just said, "but that doesn't mean that it won't happen." The problem is you didn't read, and you allowed your kind heart to negate the facts I'm 42 as of writing this book and I have yet to hit the big screen. That is a fact. Am I disappointed? Hell yes!!!, I am. I moved across the country in hopes of making my dream come true, like a million of other people in Hollywood. But YOU just can't allow me to be disappointed.

It's almost like we as people don't realize it is disappointments that have inspired anything great in this world. Who's the guy that cut off his ear and painted the picture of the guy. He was disappointed by love and obviously a little crazy. (I mean I'll cut you off before I cut a part of me off. Ain't no dick that damn good, and it's some good dick out here.)

My point is that life is inspired by people who have had enough and had faced moments when they were unhappy with the outcomes. Life is a shit show sometimes. One thing happens and then another, and another. Its Gods way of keeping things interesting, I think. He keeps it real interesting for Black people though, but I'm not going to go there. In fact, let me. I have this friend we'll call him Patrick. Patrick had been working at this Law Firm, he was the top Lawyer at his firm. He made that firm millions of dollars.

As time went on, he saw the many diverse faces that used to inhabit the firm dwindle until he was the only chocolate in the crowd or as my mother would say, "The roach in a bowl of rice." He had heard that they were looking to make someone a partner and his name was at the top of the list.

After months of waiting to hear word about whether he had made partner or not. He found out that a guy that had been there for two years and hadn't landed as many clients as he had, had gotten the partnership. I'm sure that I don't have to tell you he was devastated. I was devastated for him.

He was in the bathroom taking a much-needed deuce, (Yes, people take shits in public bathrooms in real life, even in books.) when he found out that he was never even an option. "There was no way they were going to let him be partner, he's Black.," he heard as he wiped his ass.

Patrick had done his best to play the game. He had done all the White prerequisites. Code switch, never eat chicken, denounce watermelon, make sure that his coworkers knew that BET and Tyler Perry was beneath him, and he voted for Trump. (Okay, he didn't vote for him, but he told everybody he did. He wasn't that deep down the rabbit hole. He even married a White woman in Martha's Vineyard and invited everybody. (Her parents didn't show up. They claimed they had made other plans before the date was announced. Really?)

Like I said he had done everything that he was supposed to do only to be disappointed in the end. Patrick had made himself as "White Appealing" as he could because he had been taught that that's what he needed to do. (Hell, he wasn't even attracted to White women, or women for that matter. No, he wasn't gay he was A-Sexual, look it up.

Patrick's expectation was that if he lived this life that was laid out in front of him, he would get the things that he wanted. In the end he was thoroughly disappointed and in need of a therapist because he had more problems than just disappointment.

When I got a chance to catch up with him one day, he spoke of how he felt that he had wasted 10 years of his life and his sanity working to make them one of the top firms in LA and this is what he had to show for it.

I could tell that all of this had hurt him deeply. I wanted to hug him and tell him that everything would be ok. (We ain't that type of friends,) I said, How do you feel about working there now?" He said, I hate every moment." "I said, "Well quit and start your own firm.," and guess what, he didn't. He went back to work and won more cases and to this day still works for that firm. (He ain't even a junior partner.)

I was a little disappointed by that but soon I realized some people are worker bees who need someone to give them directions and others are free thinkers who give directions. Just because I would take that step doesn't mean that he would. There are things about what I do now that I'm not willing to change, so I can't judge him for not wanting to, at least out loud that is.

I am of the thought that maybe only 2% of the truly racist people born in the 50's, 60's has actually changed their mind and ways. The rest are just waiting for the right opportunity to call you a nigger. So, I doubt if he will ever see partner.

Though Patrick lives in a cycle of disappointment, it's functional disappointment. Yes, he's unhappy but he's going to push through. Come on, we all live in some form of functional disappointment, a terrible job, marriage, divorce, writing career, bad ass kids, being single at 40, there's always something.

But for some reason in a life of disappointment we the living find a way to get by day by day. I don't know why they don't mention disappointment as one of the building blocks of life. It should be right there at the top like a blaring beacon. It inspires some of us to live out our wildest fantasies and others to fall into a state of despair.

Whatever disappointment may happen to you, just remember that it is one of the somethings that you will have to face, so get through it to come out the other side smarter, better, and faster. That's my advice, you'll thank me for it later.

Chapter

12

Bring your ass out the closet.

*F*irst ladies I don't know if your man is gay unless I don fucked him. In that case, yes ma'am he is, now
what? You gon stay with him until you have more proof or
until he embarrasses you. You shouldn't ask questions you
really don't want the answer to.

Now that that is out of the way. When I was a very
young man my mother, father, and everybody I came in
contact with could tell you, "That boy's going to be gay." As
much as I tried to hide it, it was as the song says, "written
all over my face, I didn't have to say a word." It was in everything that I did. So much so, that I didn't even realize that
I was doing anything.

Believe it or not there are those of us that just don't
have the option of hiding who we are. We were just born
more effeminate than others. Trying to hide it has never
been an option and keep in mind I'm not even on the fur-
thest scale of femininity.

There are many different versions of gay and none
of us just fit in one of them. You have your RuPaul's to this
fine ass barista at this "Starbucks I'm sitting at. Gay comes
in so many different flavors. Black, White, Asian, Mexican,
Indian, Native American and the list goes on. No, not just

137

your hairdressers and makeup artist. A lot of blue collar, white collar, celebs, and high-powered executives play ball on my field. (I wish I would have known this when I was coming up.)

Back when I was coming up, being gay was a "catch on the street and kill you offence." (Yes, young people it was just that bad.) There weren't as many laws as you have now that protected our right to just exist. We had to be ever vigilant and find the baddest "I'll hit a nigga in the face ass bitches" to hang with. Those were the girls that you know if the shit hit the fan, she was going to be fighting right next to you. Some of you women recognize this girl as the one you have to ask yourself "Why is she so rough and tumble?"

It wasn't until I decided that whenever someone would ask me was I gay, I would just say "yes." That's when all the craziness stopped. I had peace on that front, and it caused the people around me to be peaceful.

I know that that's not the case for everyone. Some people's families have cast them out, claiming to be ashamed of them and telling them that they were not worthy of love. I can understand that it can be very painful when you are young but when you are grown its harder for me to understand.

I'm of the school where love is everything, and if you're not loving on me, as me, when I'm being me then I just don't come around you. This is a sign your parents need to look out for. Not just your child being gay, but if your child doesn't share their life with you, it could be because whatever it is about their life that's keeping them away, you might not like.

It always bothers me when people say, "I don't know why my child doesn't talk to me." It's like they don't know that the walls were established by them. That everything that they are experiencing was of their own doing.

For eons, in the name of protection, parents have tried to shield their children from as many pitfalls as they could. The problem is, some of those shields while keeping the bad out, keeps the bad in. When we were coming up sex and porn and all the rest of the debauchery, we all know, and love wasn't as accessible. Nowadays almost everything is an advertisement for pleasure. What person, place or thing doesn't like pleasure?

New age parents see these things and say I have to put these walls around my child to protect him/her from all of this. The very things that you yourself take pleasure in. Most people learn most of their bad habits from the people closest to them, right inside the very same walls you put up to protect them.

These walls that you have established become problems for innocents like me, who are trying to be happy with yo son, I have to jump through so many DL hoops that I lose interest. As someone who is free to be who I am, it's really hard when you have to sit at a table and pretend that you're someone's roommate when this man just got finished dicking you down in the car in your driveway.

I gave up trying to live in somebody else's box. I wanted to know what my own box looked like. I spent years attempting to discover what kind of gay I was, (Believe me I went through a whole Crayola box before I settled on one. I look at it as a part of discovering who you are as a gay man.)

My mother was the main reason I waited to come out. I knew if I came out to her, she was going to tell my father, who I was not going to come out to.

Before I told her I did a tester, and I told my aunt who in turn told my mother who in turn sat with me on the couch like she didn't know what I was going to say. As I told her, she then asked me "Why you tell Erma Lee before you told me, I'm yo mama." My mother was more upset with the fact that she was not the first person I told than anything else.

After about a month we were back on track, but it was after that that I could live free. There is so much weight that falls off when you are living authentically. The painful reality in life is that there are many people who will never know that feeling. In a lot of cases because they haven't accepted their homosexuality themselves. When they look in the mirror they don't understand what it is that they see.

Everybody in the closet ain't there because of their family, some of these closets are self-imposed. Now a days most people don't give a hell what you do in your bedroom, or probably want to know what your "Onlyfans" handle is. This is not to say that the world has become suddenly not so bothered by homosexuality, but just to say that it's a little easier to be "Gay" now. I for one am glad that I'm alive to see these times. There were some touch-and-go moments.

You still have those people that want to keep up appearances. They see their homosexuality as a weakness and therefore they rebel against all things apparently gay even though they are in the back alley getting banged out by their homeboy and his homies, or the neighbor you wave at every morning.

Some people will tell you they're in the studio, or they're out on a hunting trip with their bros but in reality, they're doing a tour of all the bathhouses in America. (I don't make the news; I just report it.) These are the men at all those woke poets talk about and snap their fingers to in disgust at coffee houses around the world but don't realize that they created.

Women you set the pace. Men want women and in their pursuit of women, most men know that masculinity is the key. I don't care what you deny, but for the most part no woman wants a weak non-assertive man, (Hell, I don't want one). You down talk hyper-masculinity, but you secretly crave it when it's needed to protect your virtue.

Men want to get the girl, so they poke out their chest to make sure they out show all the cock in the coupe. They want you to see theirs the best. All of this cock showing has bled into the general populous and the gays have gone wild with it. Feeling a need to prove just how masculine they are.

We are all trained to find someone that we can be better than, you don't believe me? Some of you right now are in competition with a sibling, or a coworker and don't even know it. It is the way of the world to pit us against each other, so that we stay in our place and don't reach too far. You spend all this time fighting for something just because there's someone to fight against. When you don't even want what you're fighting for.

I know you just said what? Some DL, (Down Low) and hypermasculine men are fighting to look like the man that wants a woman, when in reality, they don't. This attracts three kinds of people; feminine men, women and others that don't really want to be found out. (Keep in mind gay is a spectrum, so nothing is everybody.)

Since some men are told they must be Alpha when they aren't naturally. They act out in ways that they think will constantly prove just how masculine they are. The way that they do that is by demeaning and harassing and in a lot of cases abusing the weaker of the sex.

I have this friend Avery; Avery and I went to college together for the brief 3 semesters I was there. Avery was very popular, he stayed in the gym like it was a second home. His body and very manly walk caused all the ladies to swoon when he would come around. Avery had no problem entertaining, said ladies, even though he was beating my guts out every chance that he got.

One night we were seen out eating at a regular bar in Hollywood and word got around that Avery might be gay. This threatened Avery's social-standing, and Avery couldn't have that. He made up this elaborate tale about he and I being related, and I was helping him study. The reason why we never said anything about it was because he was embarrassed. This backfired on him because he said this right on the cusp of an awakening in social behavior as it pertained to how gays were treated.

Avery thought that him saying that would make the girls say, "I understand." Instead, they said, "That's yo family. If anybody you are supposed to be there for them." (I won). Avery lost all his cool factor, with the crowd that he thirsted for acceptance from. That's not to say that everybody jumped ship. It is to say though that to rely on homophobia is just, "So Yesterday." Everybody ain't on your team anymore. That's the one good thing that came out of this cancel culture society we live in.

Being a turd to people just cause they are some kind of different just won't be tolerated. People now recognize that everybody has something different going on. Why be an ass about it? We now see gay couples in Cheerios

144

commercials and on our primetime television and they aren't being demonized for being that way. I absolutely love that I got to live in this time.

Coming out of the closet is no longer a hindrance to success, in fact it might even be what gets you in the door. My advice is to make safe places for your children. Don't lose them to the streets because you closed the front door. Be a parent to your little Lesbian, Gay, Bi, Trans, Queer, plus child so that they

can make you proud, we generally do.

Chapter 13

When they die.

"They were here and then they weren't."

Gregory D. Alexander

*T*here is no good in talking about life if you are not going to talk about death. There are few things in life more inevitable then good ole death. It's the one thing that every living thing is going to do at some point, well maybe not those Galapagos turtles they seem to live forever. Some say there are some as old as four hundred years old. I don't know that I want to live that long, but I don't want to face deaths cold handshake. (I feel like I'd be like, "Oh, hey death I think you meant to stop next door." He'd take a second look at my address plate and say, "You know what, I think your right." Then he'd go about his business.)

I don't think that any of us are ready to die. Even when it seems like we should be. I think we hold out hope that our body will say not me, not today, not until they give me a second season of "Gilmore Girls a year in the Life" or Michelle Obama becomes president. (I still hold out hope.)

We always feel like there's something that we still have to do. There's an apology we still must make in order to make things right before we go. I'm petty, if you messed with me or were an asshole before I passed, I would never give you the satisfaction of knowing that I forgave you. You will go to your grave thinking that I still hated your guts. I'm not big on forgiving people for wrongdoing.

You see the masses have told us that holding on to loathing someone effects your energy. I'm here to tell you that's a non-proven wives tale. I can hate your guts and be just fine. You think all the racist people in those "hang a nigga pictures" were rot with turmoil as their days went on, no. They went on doing and being them. This law of reciprocity that we have been told to believe is a bunch of bullshit.

When I die, I will rest knowing that the people that I don't like, I had good damn reason not to. So, I won't be holding on to things that I didn't do. On the other hand, a lot of you have lived lives where you didn't do your thing. You didn't go to France or Greece, or that bathhouse in New York where you could have caught the "Rhea," but it would have all been worth it for the amount of Puerto Rican dick you would have taken that night.

The repression of your wants is why you are saying moments before you close your eyes for the last time, "I wish I would have." I have lived my life experiencing it. I have done what I wanted to do and hopefully left a mark in someone's heart along the way. Though I don't want to die right at this moment, I guess I would be okay with it.

I believe that for some it is the uncertainty of what's to come after. A lot of people play like they know that there is a heaven or hell, but truthfully, we don't know a damn thing. I mean really you are a human being, meaning that for the most part you have probably done something fucked up to someone in your lifetime.

How many of us do you really think are going to be standing at the gates of heaven? I have said this before in one of my one man shows. I'm going to hell. There is no amount of forgiveness for some of the fucked-up shit I don did and said. Let's be honest should Jeffery Dahmer really be in heaven just because right before he died, he asked for forgiveness? (I mean, come on.)

What is really going to happen to us when we die? It's the question that has plagued the human race for centuries. Nobody really knows. It sounds good to say we will be with our lord and make cheesy obituaries from the company printer with cloud's, angel wings and staircases with light pouring them pictures, depicting us as if we were so saintly.

People, if there is a God, he knows that you killed that elephant that was minding its business on that hunting trip. He knows that you where fucking the mailman while your husband/wife was at work. He knows that you neglected your children and bought them bargain bin clothing to wear on the first day of school causing them to be demeaned their whole childhood (Sorry that was a little personal.)

Being a good person is a really hard mask to wear. Life presents you with so many opportunities to be, "not so good." I try my darndest to own up to being wrong when I am, and not let being wrong about one thing define my life. That why I don't have a lot of regrets. I take life as it is presented, not as I want it to be.

Living your life with regrets about things you didn't do is useless. I want to die knowing that I uncovered every stone and shot my shot with Winston Duke. All else life will figure out. I don't have the time or energy to regret. Death is running up faster than a homeless person outside a restaurant, and I want to be happy while I'm on this earth so that I'm not a miserable dead person.

Now let's talk about the death of someone you love. This is something different only because you are left with the emptiness and loss of the person. It's the realization that you will never have that person physically in your presence again. I was going to say that you will never hear that person say "hello" again but with modern technology we can hear that person and even see them, (that's shit is creepy, right?)

Throughout the life of a person, we create these bonds with things that are sometimes ungodly and those losses of those people, places or things can leave an unfillable hole in your life. When my mom died, I had been expecting it for years. The life she led was not a healthy one. I knew it would happen; it was just about when. You would think with me knowing this that I would have been more prepared. The truth is, you are never prepared to hear, "Gregory they found your mother dead."

Hearing that someone you have loved your whole entire life is just gone, and you didn't even get a chance to say goodbye is life altering. If you are a child that was super close to your parent it's even worse. For me there is no love I have ever had for anything that compares to how much I loved my mother. And that women got on my got damn nerves. She did things that I just didn't understand, but I loved her anyway.

Year's after she has left this earth, I still feel her coursing through my body. I say and do things just like her. I could move a certain way and know she did that. I have moments in my adult life that I wish that I could call her and say, "What you doing?," not really caring and making up

151

some reason to get off the phone but just to know that she was there. Now I'm not saying that I didn't love my father, because, I did and do, it's just a different kind of love. I wish that I could make sense of it, but it just is.

That's why in a previous chapter I talked about the bond of a man and his mother. They will always be the queen no matter how you feel. For me if my mother didn't like you, we probably wasn't going to work out in the first place. (That's cause my mother liked everybody, until she didn't like you no more, Like me.) There is this feeling of a loss of protection when your mother dies. It's like the one thing that shielded you from yourself and the other terrible pitfall of life is gone. It's a very hard pill to swallow.

I have never experience someone I loved romantically dying while I was still romantically connected to them. I have, however had two ex's who have passed on. Because of the circumstances in which we broke up, that effected how I responded to their passing. (As I have said many times in this book, I'm not perfect nor do I seek perfection, it's too hard.)

I couldn't imagine waking up one morning next to a cold dead body. (Wow that went dark, really fast.) This is the reality for many people. The person that they have spent their life with has up and passed away in their sleep.

They went to sleep thinking about all that they had to do the next day. They woke up thinking how am I going to go on without this person? (Honestly, I don't think that I could ever sleep in that bed again.)

You remember when I told you that death was inevitable, it is, but death all of a sudden, I think is harder than anything else, because it is completely unexpected. If your mate is on life support, that's considered a warning that something may happen. Your husband dying on a Peloton machine trying to beat his yesterday's miles (IE And Just Like That) is something different. I swear to you I did not see that coming. (RIP Mr. Bigg) There are a whole different set of emotions that happen and also a whole set of problems for some.

I have this friend Franny. Franny had met Lucy on a dating site. For eight months everything was amazing. They were taking trips, meeting each other's families, and planning a life together. It had seemed like Franny was really with the person she was supposed to spend the rest of her life with. While vacationing the love of Franny's life, trying to take a selfie of the skyline fell off the side of a building.

Franny was devastated. I mean who wouldn't be. Lucy who went by Lou had just proposed to Franny and they had been living together. Now all of that was done and over. (I was going to insert a joke about how fast lesbians move in relationships but due to the subject matter, I'll save it.) I and all of Franny's friends attempted to gather around her and show her that she was loved and had support, but truth is nothing we offered made a difference.

As friends you want to jump in and say that one thing that you think is going to comfort, but truthfully death is a pain that you have to work through. There are no easy fixes. You have to cry and scream and hurt until it makes no sense for you yourself to feel that way anymore. I think that we have to learn as a people that the pain you work through is not about someone else, it's about you. Your Feelings, your reactions, I mean come on you are the person going through the shit.

I had a friend tell me that they were trying their best not to blame their partner for dying and leaving them alone, but that's how they felt. I asked, "why, why are you not allowed to feel the way that you feel." As much as we like to think that love is the strongest thing in our arsenal. The government and the world has taught us that hey, it's not. Hate is the strongest emotion we have. Hate can make a celebration of life, a funeral. Hate can turn a concert in Vegas to the last place you were seen alive.

If you have to use hate in this case to get over something or get clarity, its what's necessary for you to heal. I know you're like, "What!?" Open your mind. People have coping mechanisms. Things that they use to get them through stuff. Of course, they don't hate the person for dying, but it's what they need to say to feel better. It's the way that their mind wants to get through their issue. You may not think that way. You might be a, "Don't worry you'll get through it," kind of person. Some are not. Let others feel their kind of way about their kind of pain. I assure you when you are not around, and the lights are off and they are dealing with what they are going through you're not feeling it. Grieving loss internally is a solo activity. Sure, external comfort can help, but when it all comes down to it that person has got to learn to breathe again on their own.

You really only have two options in life, to live or to die. Most people wake up choosing the first, but a lot of people don't have the option. The bonds that they have developed are just too strong.

My friend Gretchen and I were at Tender Greens having a meal when she got a call from her mother. She decided to avoid the call and continue the trivial conversation that we were having. Gretchen's Father had died about two months prior, and she had really gotten tired of her mother just not wanting to do anything but cry over the phone or in person. She said to me, "Greg I just need a break. I loved my father too, but it's too much. The house is dark, she barely washes her ass, and I just don't know how long I can put up with it."

I thought about when my father died. My mother and father were not together but as my mother talked at my father's funeral it was obvious to anyone looking and listening on that my father was the love of my mother's life. Not the man she was currently dating. (If it sounds like there's some animosity there, there is. Another story for another time.) Gretchen and her mother had already had a somewhat strained relationship. Something about that mother daughter thing that never quite mixes well.

We finished our food and parted ways. About three hours later Gretchen calls me and says she has found her mother in bed dead after taking a bottle of sleeping pills. She left a note saying that she just couldn't take it anymore. Gretchen was devastated and to this day still thinks that if she had of just answered the phone her mother would still be alive. That is a heavy burden to carry. It's a lil irrational to me, but as I said you have to allow people to feel the way that they feel.

One of the best things that my father ever taught me was that some people are waiting on their ticket and

others just go ahead and buy it. He wasn't talking about suicide in that scenario, but it still applies. As bad as we think it
is, it's still an option that people choose. As someone who
has attempted and failed at it, to get to that point, you have
to feel like there is nothing more than you can do. Nothing
is easing this pain that never subsides inside of you. Your
only option is to take your life.

Most people who commit suicide just don't want to
feel anymore. There's levels to this shit people. You are sitting around saying, "oh that was dumb, why would they do
that?" only people who have never been pushed to that
point will ask that question. For the person that is doing it, it
is very apparent why they are doing it, and at that point
they don't give a fuck that you won't understand why. Got
damnit people, it's not aways about you, and how you feel
about what someone is doing.

Ultimately a person will just wait on their ticket or
buy it, and it will not have had anything to do with you. I say
spend more time loving on a person at this time, because
the shit is hard. Support in times like this is not always
about what you can say and judgement. Sometimes it's just
about being there. Not offering words, but shoulders and
sympathy.

I will never be able to talk about all the niche cases of dealing with the loss of someone, but I can say this, well take this quote, "Every storm runs out of rain." Just when you think that you will never be able to pull through, you do. It's the funny way that life works. You will laugh again, and the funny thing is you might even be the person telling the jokes.

To my father who passed away in 2000 and my mother in 2013. I still feel the sting of your loss every day. As I have written this book your voices have spilled from my fingers. Life lessons and quotes and just who I am all around is because you loved me. I was able to step into my life without you because you gave me the tools both genetically and externally to survive.

I love you.

Greg

In Closing

*T*hough there are many more topics about which I could

talk. I think this is enough for now, and besides if I talked about all the topics now, what would I have to talk about in my next book? I can't tell you all my secrets, some of you might use them against me, and I can't have that.

In short, I hope that what you got out of this book is the need to be aware of everything around you. We no longer live in a world where everything is up and downside to side. You can spend your life pretending that your bubble is all that there is in the world, but the reality is it's not.

I hope that you have learned something. Remember every subject matter does not apply to you. You are not the only person in the world to talk about. So shut up, have a child, suck a dick, do a threesome, enjoy cuddle season with a big boy, tell your daughter she's a bitch, because she has it coming, or ask your partner for the sex you deserve. Do it all for the rest of the world because we tired of your frowsy ass.

Thank you: I love you, Bye, Bye

Greg

The Truth about Love, life, and Sex

Made in the USA
Las Vegas, NV
09 September 2024

95052162R00095